TAGGART SIEGEL has been directing award-winning documentaries and dramas for more than 25 years. Reflecting cultural diversity with absorbing style, his films bring compelling voices and visions to a global audience. From spiritual elders struggling to preserve traditions in alien environments to marginalized youth surviving hostile streets, his films present vital perspectives rarely seen in mainstream media. *The Real Dirt on Farmer John* won 31 International Film Festival awards. His latest film *Queen of the Sun: What Are the Bees Telling Us?*, winner of ten international awards, is currently being released around the world. (See further at www.queenofthesun.com) Taggart is the Executive Director of Collective Eye, Inc. (www.collectiveeye.com), a non-profit media organization based in San Francisco and Portland, Oregon.

JON BETZ is an award-winning documentary filmmaker and the producer of *Queen of the Sun*. He is a graduate of Rhode Island School of Design, where he received the Tiffany Rosen Scholarship Award for Excellence in Narrative Filmmaking and the Fine Arts Award for Excellence in Film. Jon's work strives to maintain a high degree of artistic craft whilst digging deeply into the spiritual, emotional and ethical issues surrounding his characters. His previous film *Memorize-you-saw-it* is an intimate auto-biographical documentary journal of his time as an aid worker with former child soldiers in Eastern Uganda. Jon is Director of Collective Eye, Inc.

D1730733

QUEEN OF THE SUN

What Are the Bees Telling Us?

An anthology compiled by Taggart Siegel and Jon Betz

CLAIRVIEW

Clairview Books
Hillside House, The Square
Forest Row, RH18 5ES

www.clairviewbooks.com

Published by Clairview 2011

*The publishers offer special thanks to poet laureate Carol Ann Duffy for her generous permission to include
'Virgil's Bees' in this anthology*

A catalogue record for this book is available from the British Library

ISBN 978 1 905570 34 8

Cover photo by Ruby Bloom; cover artwork by Monet Molina
(adapted for this book by Andrew Morgan Design)
Typeset by DP Photosetting, Neath, West Glamorgan
Interior layout and design by S.E. Gulbekian
Printed and bound in Malta by Gutenberg Press Ltd.

CONTENTS

FOREWORD

Honeybees have inspired man since time immemorial. We admire them not only for the delicious fruits of their labours, but also for their labour itself. These days they are working harder than ever, as they struggle to survive; and the odds against their survival are increasingly stacked against them, as man's ways of working against Nature threaten to defeat them. Industrial agriculture has become a form of warfare against the natural world, producing food of questionable nutritional value and at enormous cost to the natural environment. In such man-made landscapes, the bees have no choice but to collect pollen that poisons their young. They have no choice but to suck nectar from the corrupted flowers that blossom in the monocultural deserts which we have created — stark symbols of our estrangement from Nature and our alienated souls.

Revered once as messengers of the gods and celebrated in all ancient cultures, the bees have been subjected increasingly over the last 150 years to the laws of the market, as trade in their 'products' — and even in the bees themselves — has grown into a vast global industry. The children of the sun have been dragged down to earth. We keep them in square boxes and approach them as if suited for warfare. We rob them to stack the shelves of our supermarkets with their precious honey, feeding them sugar instead. Every facet of the spiritual life of the hive has been deconsecrated to suit the imperatives of commerce. Is it any wonder

that the bees are sick? We look to science to explain their sickness, but the remedies for their sickness — which is our sickness too — will not be found in laboratories.

As human beings endowed with spirit, we can choose to change. Of course, science can give us new insights into the wonders of the honey bee, about which we still understand so little. Public opinion and the media can help also: witness the success of the campaign led by biodynamic beekeeper Thomas Radetzki, culminating in the recent decision by the European Court of Justice to ban European imports of GMO-contaminated honey. This is a victory not only for beekeepers and consumers, but also for the bees.

Art is yet another powerful instrument of change. In Britain the bees have found a modern patron saint in the Poet Laureate (who is also Patron to the Natural Beekeeping Trust). Carol Ann Duffy's poems about bees are exquisitely beautiful, and suffused with a deep understanding of the hive's mysteries. 'The hive is love, what we serve, preserve, avowed in Latin murmurs as we come and go, skydive, freighted with light...', she writes in one of the poems in her new volume *The Bees*. These poems are invitations to the reader and listener to ponder the bee and the life of love in the hive.

Give and take, the bees are telling us. Take care of us and we shall continue to keep the world in fruit and flower. If we listen to them with our hearts, as our

ancestors did, we shall be sure to find our lives enriched and ensouled. The essays in this book, and the film *Queen of the Sun* itself, are an excellent contribution to this endeavour. They speak in a rich diversity of voices, but the common message is clear: reconnect with Nature and Nature will reconnect with us.

It is easy to become defeatist, but the bees themselves are challenging us to be optimistic and to act. In the final sequence of the film, biodynamic beekeeper Gunther Hauk says: 'I have hope, to the last flower, the last bee'. We should all aspire to become stewards of the earth. Let us imagine a world in which bees can live and bestow their gifts on us freely.

Heidi Herrmann
Director, Natural Beekeeping Trust

VIRGIL'S BEES

Carol Ann Duffy

Bless air's gift of sweetness, honey
from the bees, inspired by clover,
marigold, eucalyptus, thyme,
the hundred perfumes of the wind.
Bless the beekeeper

who chooses for her hives
a site near water, violet beds, no yew,
no echo. Let the light lilt, leak, green
or gold, pigment for queens,
and joy be inexplicable but there
in harmony of willowherb and stream,
of summer heat and breeze,

each bee's body
at its brilliant flower, lover-stunned,
strumming on fragrance, smitten.

For this,
let gardens grow, where beelines end,
sighing in roses, saffron blooms, buddleia;
where bees pray on their knees, sing, praise
in pear trees, plum trees; bees

Are the batteries of orchards, gardens, guard them.

INTRODUCTION:
HOW WE CAME TO MAKE THE FILM

Taggart Siegel and Jon Betz

The beauty of the seed is that out of one you can get millions. The beauty of the pollinator is that it does the work of turning that one into a million. And that's an economics of abundance, of renewability, an economics of mutuality. That to me is the real economics of growth. Because life means growth and abundance.

Dr. Vandana Shiva

Last night as I was sleeping,
I dreamt – marvellous error! –
that I had a beehive
here inside my heart,
And the golden bees
were making white combs
and sweet honey
from my old failures.

Antonio Machado (1875–1939)

By the fall of 2006, mainstream books and magazine articles about Colony Collapse Disorder and the decline of honey bees were appearing in large numbers. Many such articles featured a quote attributed to Einstein – 'If bees disappeared from the surface of the globe, humanity would only have four years left to live.' Though there is some dispute whether Einstein actually said this, there is a large body of evidence to show our huge dependence on pollinators, and the dire risk to many ecosystems if they were to vanish. As Gunther Hauk, a biodynamic beekeeper featured in the film, *Queen of the Sun: What Are the Bees Telling Us?*, says, 'Bees nurture and sustain life on earth.'

I had never realized the magnitude of what it would mean for honey bees to disappear. These articles were a major wake-up call. Without a major shift in our approach to agriculture and the natural world, I realized we would be passing this crisis onto the next generation – including my three-year-old daughter Olive – and letting it grow to unimaginable consequences.

The next four years of my life were dedicated to research, fundraising, filming, editing and distribution with my producer Jon Betz who has played a crucial and integral part in making *Queen of the Sun: What Are the Bees Telling Us?* We felt it was our responsibility to communicate the gravity of the bee crisis to a wide global audience, and introduce the unsung heroes struggling to save honey bees, whose perspectives are often excluded by mainstream media. Making *Queen of the Sun* took us on a journey through the catastrophic disappearance of bees and into the mysterious world of the beehive. The film explores the 15,000-year history of beekeeping, illuminating the deep sense

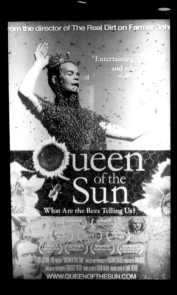

OW SHOWING

NOW SHOWING

NOW SH

from the director of The Real Dirt on Farmer John

"Entertaining,
and rele

Queen
of the
Sun

What Are the Bees Telling Us?

WWW.QUEENOFTHESUN.COM

WILL F

EVERY
MUST

of affinity humans have historically had with bees, and showing how that relationship of respect and reverence has been superseded by highly mechanized industrial practices.

Queen of the Sun became an in-depth investigation to uncover the alarming underlying causes of Colony Collapse Disorder, as well as possible solutions to the crisis. Inspired by Rudolf Steiner's lectures on bees in 1923, *Queen of the Sun* sought out the voices and visions of biodynamic and organic beekeepers, philosophers and scientists around the world, all intent on helping honey bees to survive.

In the context of rising media alarm about the worldwide collapse of bee colonies, scientists are hunting for an illusory silver bullet to cure CCD and preserve a multi-billion dollar industry. They have yet to locate their culprit. Some articles report theories that a bacterium and a virus may be causing CCD. These articles fail to mention the wider range of issues such as pesticides, GMOs, exploitative beekeeping practices and other factors, focusing instead on the most immediate symptoms rather than underlying causes. This is where documentary film is a powerful medium. In an age where news media have been corrupted by corporate control, independent documentaries remain vital for uncovering issues that plague or threaten our world. There are many vested interests that seem willing to sacrifice the planet's long-term sustainability for immediate profit. This iron grip of commercialism has led, for instance, to the trucking of huge numbers of bees thousands of miles to pollinate (heavily sprayed) almond crops in the US, or to 'tricking' the bee by means of synthetic pheromones into increasing their foraging activities. More and more labour is required of these insect slaves, under ever worse and more toxic conditions. Migratory beekeeping exists because of monoculture. As Michael Pollan states, 'Three-quarters of all bees in America come to the almond orchards in California to pollinate the almonds, where they have to be strengthened with high-fructose corn syrup. If there's anything more viscerally offensive, it's the idea of feeding the creators of honey high-fructose corn syrup.' He also explains that migratory beekeeping contributes to the spread of disease between bees: 'That's where all of the bees of America mix. We've created a bee bordello. Monoculture is the reason that bees are dying.' It's also worth remembering that bees attune subtly to their local surroundings, and co-evolve with its distinctive features. To tear the bees from their local fabric and truck them long distances must inevitably be a shock to their system.

This story is made more tragic by the fact that these innocent pollinators are helping the world to flourish and stay in bloom, and yet are being so maltreated. Johannes Wirz, microbiologist and biodynamic beekeeper at the Goetheanum in Switzerland eloquently states, 'I start to see the flight of the bees as a golden thread in the landscape, weaving from flower to flower ... If bees are dying, we can be sure that butterflies are dying too, that solitary bees and bumble bees will be dying; and we know from academic studies of ecology that if insects are dying, then birds and plants will also die.'

What we are doing to the bees, we are really doing to ourselves. Bees are a window on our larger relationship with nature. 'Colony collapse,' says Gunther Hauk, 'is the bill we are getting for all we have done to the bees.' Sawing off the branch we are sitting on is therefore a fairly apt metaphor for the ways in which we are endangering a life-sustaining insect, to which we ourselves owe so much. The bees are a barometer of the health of the world, and fly millions of miles in their pollination labours. As Michael Pollan says in *Queen of the Sun*, 'The relationship of bees and flowers is one of the most beautiful co-evolutionary relationships we have. Bees are the legs of plants.' Quite apart from pollination, bees have provided humans with honey, food, medicine and wax for over 15,000 years. Yet the bond between humans and bees has now changed drastically from a deeply felt affinity to profit-driven exploitation.

Rudolf Steiner, an Austrian scientist, philosopher and social innovator, predicted the collapse of the pollinator population as long ago as the 1920s, during seven lectures to beekeepers and workers at the Goetheanum in Switzerland. He stated that mechanized and industrialized beekeeping practices, including artificial queen breeding, could lead to the demise of the bee within 80 to a 100 years. During the 85 years since Steiner made his prediction, commercial beekeeping practices of the kind he lamented have become standard, not to mention widespread use of toxic pesticides and now also gene technology whose risks are still unquantifiable. In the last 14 years, the world has lost a staggering 70 to 90 percent of its bee colonies. This dire loss will affect us all, not least the commercial interests of agro-business.

There is probably no single cause of Colony Collapse Disorder, but rather a dangerous cocktail of problems. Steiner was particularly concerned, in his day, with the artificial breeding of queens. Due to such practices, queen bees that used to live four to six years now sometimes live only from six months to one year. Gunther Hauk believes we have to raise queens again the natural way, and that the only means for our own survival is by putting the health of other living beings on a par with our own. This respectful attitude to the natural world is one echoed here also by Vandana Shiva, who stresses how essential it is to recognize the vital contribution and interdependency of all creatures on earth.

As we made the film, it was staggering for us to realize how many commercial beekeepers are treating hives with artificial chemicals and feeding their bees corn syrup. Beekeepers are using antibiotics and miticides to fight bacteria and pests. Antibiotics are leaching into the honey, and causing humans to become resistant. The varroa mite, a blood-sucking scourge of bees, has adapted to these chemical agents and developed resistance to them to become a 'super-mite'. Through our historical connection with honey bees, and our recent debilitating interventions, honey bees have become almost entirely dependent on us. Gunther Friedmann, a German biodynamic (Demeter) beekeeper in the film says that without our care only very few bee colonies will survive. After learning how we have maltreated the bees, it is daunting to realize the responsibility we must now shoulder to remedy the situation and restore their equilibrium and health.

Yet Gunther Hauk is clear that every crisis contains an opportunity, and that the 'future can be born' from it. Hauk, who founded Spikenard Farm honey bee sanctuary says, 'Turning this crisis around is not going to be easy and it won't happen overnight. The bees are telling us to become true caretakers, and the only solution is by creating surroundings of wild flowers, with plentiful forage and diversity. Honey bee sanctuaries are springing up like mushrooms in this country.' People ask Hauk whether there is any hope, given the mess we are in and all we are doing to nature. He replies that he would be hopeful right up to the very last day, to the very last plant.

Horst Kornberger, likewise, who is featured in *Queen of the Sun*, speaks words of hope: 'We have to care for nature in the right way and nature will care for us in turn. So community is not just a human problem, it's a global problem, community with one another and nature.' The crisis can show us the vital interdependency with nature we have all too often overlooked, and this in turn can galvanize us to reconnect with the natural world in more conscious and healing ways.

In making *Queen of the Sun* we were inspired by discovering movements to save bees in communities across the world. Sustainable beekeepers and advocates are striving to renew a culture that takes its cues from the beehive – which is always in service to a greater cause. At the Melissa Gardens Honeybee Sanctuary, Michael Thiele, a biodynamic beekeeper, says, 'The

beehive is like a monastery. There is a striving for selflessness. All of the bees dedicate their lives to the bigger entity, the beehive.'

Such bee-nurturing communities are championing a renewal of agriculture and healthy beekeeping, as well as a cross-pollination of art, science and spirituality as Joseph Beuys, the innovative twentieth-century artist, proposed and exemplified. Einstein was right (and this quote is certainly by him): 'It is impossible to remedy a problem by using the same tools that created it.'

Our hope for the *Queen of the Sun* film and book is that they will act as a catalyst for dramatic renewal that inspires and invigorates a growing culture of human equilibrium with nature. Like the film, this book is nothing if not a collaborative project, speaking with the many voices of people working – from different perspectives, yet with a common concern – towards a hopeful future. A great many environmental films focus on the doom and gloom of pending environmental disaster, but we take heart that there is a way out, or through, if we listen to the bees. The illness itself can suggest the cure if we are attentive, active and less self-seeking; if we really understand how to place ourselves at the service of nature's wisdom, cooperating with it rather than imposing our wilfulness on it. We can learn from the bees. As Gunther Hauk says, 'The bees are the most exquisite beings. They show us what true service can be like.' The opportunity of the bee crisis is that it might force us to grow beyond our narrower self-interest to become conscious guardians and custodians of the natural world.

Part One
THE BEAUTY OF BEES

'Life in a beehive is established with extraordinary wisdom behind it ... You would be able to gain a correct and true understanding of life within the beehive if you were to allow for the fact that everything in the environment that surrounds the Earth in all directions has an extremely strong influence on what goes on in the beehive.'

Rudolf Steiner

MOVING THE BEES

Jacqueline Freeman

We're called to move the hive
out of the farmer's wall
the tiny hole 'neath the gutters
quiet and calm in the cold spring chill.

My husband at the ladder's top
skillsaws a square
and lifts the wall away
exposing sleeping bees,
long white pillars of brood
and the pale yellow pollen from
midwinter spruce blooms.

I climb the ladder with my bucket
– not for honey – I do not come to steal.
I cut the comb and carry each golden panel
20 steps down to earth
affixed to a bar in a new hive
and a safer place in our field
under pine and cedar boughs.

Leaning against the high sunny wall
I carefully grasp the row of waxy cells
as they waken, stir, then rise up
in a cloud of ten thousand bees.
The sound! The sound! Surrounding me
an electrifying moment
enfolded and embraced by the hive.

BEE CRISIS – WORLD CRISIS

Horst Kornberger

I am no expert on bees. Nor on ecology. But since experts seem set on wrecking the world, laymen must raise their voices. By profession I am an interdisciplinary artist, writer, poet and teacher. I have been involved in amateur beekeeping in western Australia, but my relation to bees is primarily an artistic one. Inspired by the artist Joseph Beuys, and seeking icons for the environmental age, I have worked with honey and wax as artistic media. Part of this search is my interest in paradigms, the way they come into being, establish themselves and claim more and more minds until they rule with undisputed power over decades, centuries and sometimes millennia.

To me the bee crisis is first and foremost a crisis of our current mindset, and I see art as one way of warming the wax of paradigm and bringing it into new shape. During my work I came across a lecture series on bees that influenced much of Beuys's work, particularly his social vision. To me the same pages that sparked Beuys's social sculpture became a doorway to a new artistic ecology. They also provided a prime catalyst for a much needed paradigm shift, as they challenge our notions of time, foresight and interconnectedness.

Researchers all over the world are trying to solve the mystery of disappearing bees. For many the varroa mite is the obvious culprit. But this mite co-existed with Asian bees long before colonies began to collapse. In fact, the long co-evolution of bees with varroa is probably key here, and will eventually be so also, hopefully, for European bees. Herbicides, pesticides and electro-smog are also in the dock and no doubt play their part. But bees are dying in areas unaffected by herbicides. Colony collapse occurs even where there is little radiation.

The 1923 lecture series that inspired Beuys predates the bee-colony collapse by some 80 years. It is rather startling to find the demise of the honey bee broached in the first lecture. The speaker (who was neither a beekeeper nor an expert as we understand it) addresses this theme as follows:

But now we come to this whole new chapter concerning the artificial breeding of bees … Much can be said for the artificial breeding of queen bees, because it does simplify things. But the strong bonding of bee generations, a bee family, will be detrimentally affected over a longer period … In certain respects you will be able only to praise artificial breeding, if all necessary precautions are taken, as Mr Mueller described to us. But we will have to wait and see how things will look after 50 to 80 years. Certain forces that have operated organically in the beehive until now

will become mechanized ... It won't be possible to establish the intimate relationship between the queen bee you have purchased and the worker bees the way it would arise all by itself in nature. But at the beginning the effects of this are not apparent...

Mr Mueller, a conventional beekeeper in the audience, had contributed to the discussion. To me he is part of the greater picture and his contribution holds metaphoric importance as a representative of modern outlooks: a practical, professional, knowledgeable expert.

Naturally this practical, knowledgeable man was very much taken aback by the speaker's statements. His reaction is understandable, particularly as the speaker blamed the practices that had made beekeeping profitable for a catastrophe nobody in the room would live long enough to see. Nor was there any evidence of it at the time.

It is obvious from what follows in the lectures that this statement remained a bone of contention for the professional Mr Mueller. Later in the series the lecturer, obviously referring to heated discussions, reiterates his statement:

Nevertheless, it is important to gain this insight – that it is one matter if you let nature take its course and only help to steer it in the right direction when necessary, but it is entirely another matter to apply artificial methods to speed things along.

I really don't want to take a strong position against what Mr Mueller has stated. It is quite correct that we can't determine these matters today; it will have to be delayed until a later time. Let's talk to each other again in 100 years Mr Mueller; then we'll see what kind of opinion you have at that point...

Whenever I read this passage I can almost hear the laughter in the room ... but I fail to join in. Hives are dying worldwide. The plight of the honey bee has become reality. If it continues, loss of honey will be the least of calamities. Bees are the agronomists of nature, ecologists in action. Along with many other insects they pollinate our major crops and are major collaborators we cannot afford to lose.

The lecturer on bees was one of the few great universalists of the last century: Rudolf Steiner, perhaps best known as the founder of Waldorf education and biodynamic farming. While I am fascinated that Steiner was able to foresee the bee collapse, point out the causes and accurately estimate the time for it to take effect, I am even more fascinated by the fact that his contribution is ignored by current researchers. To me this is a picture of the one-sided orientation of an outlook that urgently needs to change. There is something in the present paradigm that would rather suffer a crisis, no matter how devastating, than entertain the validity of a different mindset.

To me this is a metaphor in itself and as important as the bee crisis, deforestation, pollution and global warming. It points to the cause behind all these: the current paradigm and its defensive mechanisms. Science seems to rule by force of majority vote that nobody has ever consciously given. It invokes the notion that solutions are found in details and that parts make

the whole. It applies the microscope of the mind where the 'macroscope' of applied imagination is necessary. Steiner's lectures are challenging in this respect. They oppose prevailing trends with a radical re-imagining of our concept of ecology. Interestingly, Steiner's insights are per-fectly intelligible to common sense. They resonate with what we already know. They are compatible with our sense of com-passion. While it takes an expert to manage an apiary and trained scientists to fathom the chemical composition of queen sub-stance, the most important insights about bees are commonly accessible, drawing on our human capacity to connect com-passionately with nature, and in this case with the essential nature of the bee.

This essential bee is not hidden away in some unknown function of her organism. We need not know the composition of the bee's genome to apprehend her being. These details are merely the fine print to the text we can already read.

The most obvious thing about bees is their sociability. Relatedness is part of their nature and community is the essential theme of the hive. Birds live in flocks, wolves in packs, cattle in herds. However, while a single bird will survive in a cage, an isolated wolf can fend for itself, a cow on its own will not die of loneliness – a bee will. It cannot be separated from its kind, and least of all from its queen. Take a bee and keep it apart, give it ample space, water and feed. Though you tend to all its needs, it will perish. To the bee, sociability is as important as water. It is not only honey that keeps bees alive, but their connection with their queen.

The single bee cannot live without the hive. The hive cannot exist for long without the queen. Take the queen away and prevent the rearing of the successor, and the whole hive will perish: all the intricate city state, the rich stores of honey, the complex rituals of the workers, all the finely attuned and highly organized civilization will fall apart. The hive will die among abundant stores of honey, perish inside its fortress of wax, and disintegrate despite thousands of workers. Without the centrepiece of the queen, the architecture of the hive falls apart. But if the queen is restored at any point, brought back even after most of the hive has perished, when everything seems doomed, the colony will latch onto life.

We need not be an expert to appreciate the bond between bees and queen. It is obvious. All else is secondary. For the bees, life is worthwhile only as long as the queen exists and ceases to have meaning without her. Honey that matters so much to us matters little to them compared with their queen. The essential is what bees cannot live without: the all-pervading atmosphere of familiarity that links all bees to their queen. The hive and all it is and does are a result of this bond.

Queen and queen substance

The queen's life is one of continuous labour. Her sole task is the generation of brood. A queen may lay up to 1500 eggs in a day, which amounts to an egg per minute. In other words, every minute a new bee issues from her creative capabilities. She regulates the life of her offspring through queen substance, a scent she emanates from her head glands and that continuously regulates the social life of her subjects. By means of this substance the queen spreads herself over the entire colony. Her ladies-in-waiting lick this precious scent off her body and then spread it throughout the Queendom. When the workers sense this scent they know that the queen is in place, the hive is secure and the future cared for.

Every queen has her own particular scent. This royal perfume permeates the hive, linking centre with periphery and connecting the single queen with the whole hive. Queen substance is a bonding agent: a communal assurance and communication device. It is the material manifestation of the relatedness of bees.

If a foreign queen (one raised in another colony, or artificially bred) is introduced into the hive to make it more productive, bees sense her alien scent and are hostile at first. The new scent reeks of strangeness, usurpation, of a foreign and superimposed intervention. It takes time and a little 'persuasion' to make them accept the new mother. Persuasion here means to confront the hive with its own extinction. Beekeepers kill the old queen and remove all brood so that the bees are left facing their impending doom, the end of their colony. The all-important bond to the queen is broken and their future destroyed. After they have been left under this death-threat for a couple of days, the new queen is placed into the hive.

She is the bees' only hope of survival, a saviour supplied by clever design in a moment of utter distress. The bees will eventually accept her, but not immediately.

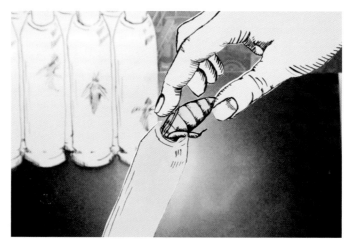

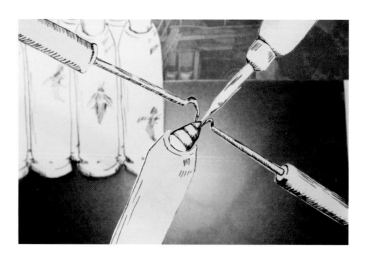

The queen is posted in a cage and in a cage she is put into the hive. Even faced with death it takes time for the bees to accept the new ruler. But accept they will, for they are doomed otherwise. Without a new mother replenishing their diminishing ranks their civilization has come to an end and their stores are useless.

But this queen is not a true queen. Her rule is not home grown. She is a surrogate-mother in terms of familiarity, a usurper in political parlance – an interloper in the fabric of the hive, cutting across the history of its hereditary strain, and rupturing essential continuity.

Until the beginning of the twentieth century queens were bred within their hive and every hive from one queen. If a queen failed, another replaced her from the same stock. All this makes for home-grown royalty and a population of unified descent. The intense relatedness so characteristic of bees is rooted in their common ancestry. Until then the social fabric of hive had rarely been broken, and queens mated in a time-honoured ritual, with regional drones adding male variety to the pure female line.

It took centuries to penetrate the reproductive secret of the queen. But whatever research brought to light was put to use. As every bit of understanding was translated into commercial benefits the semi-domesticated bee became an industrialized insect, the hive a factory and the queen a slave of profit.

The caged queen

The association between bees and industry is ancient. Bees are among the most pro-ductive beings in nature. They are symbolic of abundance achieved by communal effort. The queen was the obvious focus of this diligence. Queen and bees are a whole. She does not lord over her subjects, but makes herself subject to the whole, i.e. the hive. In some sense she is as instrumental as any other bee in the hive. And behind this hive stand all the hives before, the long history and endless lineage of bees over time.

This ancient, long-tended bond is broken every time a foreign queen is forced upon the hive. The continuity ceases. The new ruler is no home-grown queen but an imposition from without. She has no part in the history and biological tradition of the hive. She will breed bees for the hive and the hive will make honey for its keeper. It will be bee business as usual. The work will commence. The hive will survive – yet at an initially invisible but over time ever more apparent cost.

There are many variations of this procedure. But they all come down to increasing yield by breaking the bond between the queen and bees. And all this is done again and again. Bees are repeatedly orphaned and the effect is debilitating over time. The beekeeper himself, in turn, is governed by the carrot of profit dangling in front and the whip of economic pressures from behind. And all this is entirely sanctified, supported and indeed made possible by a paradigm that rules the minds of the world with an absolutism that would put Louis XIV to shame.

The formula of 'import queen and export honey' *seems* to work. Hence queen breeding has long become a thriving business of its own. Reared to maturity, the young mothers-to-be are put into a cage and then sent to apiaries, sometimes to the other side of the world. To the new hive these posted royalty bring the scent of a far-away hive mixed with strange emanations of paper and tape and transport by air and land — all anathema to the scent-sensitive bees, and to their intimately woven connections with their immediate surroundings.

Propagation has been taken from the hive. The bond between queen and bees has become commercialized. Reproduction has become business. And all seems profitable. There is more honey for more people. And more profit for more keepers. It is as convenient as it is efficient. But in all this the essential bee is overlooked. The intrinsic bee, the 'bee in all bees' comes short. The hive in all hives begins to ail.

Nature is patient, but not for ever. Bees can adjust, but not to everything. They have accepted sugary syrup instead of honey. They patiently work artificial wax foundations instead of their own comb. They fit their curved architectural artworks in prefabricated rectangular frames. All this has limited bees' self-expression. Step by step we have exploited their generous diligence for commercial gain. The breeding of queens is but the tip on the pyramid of exploitation: a slow-acting poison that attacks the essential nature of the bee. The result is the global immune disease that we call colony collapse.

To blame beekeepers is entirely beside the point. They love their hives and their jobs. They merely do what everyone else does. Their rationale is sound by conventional standards. The practice is as efficient as it can be under the circumstances. They are victims of the same paradigm we all suffer from. The bee crisis is a crisis of the global mind and we all are responsible.

We *know* more about bees than any generation before us. And yet we *understand* less about them than ever. As our eyes have been opened to detail, our minds have been closed to the whole. We have learned to decode the genome, but forgotten to heed the obvious.

Bee crisis and environmental crisis belong together. The solution for one will provide solutions for the other. Both require a new paradigm: a compassionate ecology that meets nature on her own terms; a chance for a thorough change in the way we think, feel and act. It is a message come just in time, a wind warning before the storm.

The bee crisis is a global call to action. It asks us to trust our own judgement and not leave problems to the experts who have created them. It asks us to feel with nature and suffer her violation as our own.

THE MIRACLES OF HONEY

Kerry Grefig

Honey, the nectars of a landscape miraculously transformed through the work of the honey bee, has enticed, intrigued and been revered by people since prehistoric times. But what is it about this sticky substance that is considered so precious?

Why did people write about honey in ancient holy texts such as the Indian Vedas, the Old and New Testaments, the Koran, and the Chinese Shi Jing? Why did South American Indians regard it as a gift from the gods; and Buddhists of India use it to mark the Buddha's retreat into the wild? What is so extraordinary about honey that the ancient Greeks had a god of beekeeping, Aristaeus, and Christians their own patron saint, Ambrose? Was honey, a gift worthy of offering to a god, and valued so greatly because of its capacity to aid in healing wounds?

Yes, honey is a delicious sweetener; but is that why ancient people on several continents sought perilous access to wild colonies by climbing tall trees and scaling down rock faces? Is this why it is found in the tombs of Egyptian Pharaohs? Or was it because honey is a fine cosmetic, wonderful for the skin? What was it that inspired the Egyptians to forge a relationship with the honey bee, developing from bee hunters to beekeepers?

Honey and its creator were both equally revered. The emblem of a bee was used on coins at the Greek city of Ephesus; and the Egyptians named the entire region of Lower Egypt 'Bee Land'. But why, of the millions of insects on earth, was the bee held in such universal regard?

From primeval times through to today, both honey and the bee have inspired our deep interest and admiration. How is it that a small insect and a sweet substance can have such a significant impact around the world and throughout the ages? Possibly the story of how bees make honey may reveal something to us.

Nectars transformed

In making just one pound of honey, let alone the two hundred pounds a colony can produce in a season, bees accomplish something astonishing. Honey embodies collaboration, diligence, perseverance and precision.

The story of this miraculous event of transforming floral nectar into honey begins when worker bees that have reached three weeks of age are released from their hive duties and take flight to forage for pollen and nectar. They gather pollen to meet protein, fat, vitamin and mineral requirements. However, it is the nectar they bring back that will be transformed into precious honey and used as their source of carbohydrates.

Forager bees, steadfast and committed

to their task, make up to 30 trips a day. Using their long, strawlike proboscis, they collect nectar from the wild flowers and herbs of meadows, the shrubs and trees of hillsides, and from crops of cultivated land. In one trip they visit up to 500 blossoms to fill their honey crop, an organ used to transport nectar which is separate from their digestive stomach. They freely dip into this storage unit, and shunt nectar from their crop directly to their stomach should they need food while out foraging.

Their perseverance is exemplified by their ability to fly back to the hive with a full crop, since the nectar they are carrying amounts to 85 per cent of their body-weight. An extraordinary feat! Flying with a full load, worker bees laboriously return to the hive, yet they don't rest after such effort. They transfer the nectar to a hive bee and return directly to foraging, except when they take a moment to perform their waggle dance to tell other bees of a nectar source.

While dancing on the honeycomb in this way, giving precise coordinates of the source, they recruit other foragers. The intensity of their dance is determined by the quantity and quality of the food source. To announce excellent floral resources, they dance a little longer and with greater enthusiasm.

The waggle dance can communicate the location and direction of food sources from 100 yards to two miles from the hive. The dancing bee starts by moving a semicircle in one direction, stopping, then moving in a straight line. During the straight portion of this dance, bees wag their abdomens to communicate the direction of the food source in relation to the sun. Bees wag

facing straight if the food source is in the direction of the sun and wag to the right or left if the source is to the right or left of the sun. To conclude the performance, bees dance a half circle in the other direction, finishing a figure of eight.

They present a round dance to communicate food sources 100 yards away from the hive or closer. They circle in one direction, then the other. Not as elaborate as waggle dances, round dances do not provide directional information nor do they specify the exact location of the source. The bees dance just to let other scouts know that food is close by.

After dancing, they fly back off to forage again. There is no rest while nectar is flowing and the sun is shining. Back in the hive, house bees, operating in the dark, transform the nectar into honey. The bees need to convert this substance, which is nearly 80 per cent water, consisting primarily of complex sugars, to a substance which is 17–18 per cent water, consisting of simple sugars.

This is where honey bees function as alchemists and proficient scientists. They produce an enzyme, invertase, which inverts the complex sugar of nectar (sucrose) into simple sugars (glucose and fructose). This chemical reaction actually starts in the crop of the forage bee as it transports nectar back to the hive. Though foraging bees make some modifications, the nectar they deliver to the hive is not yet honey. The hive bees now have much work to do. They start by spending about half an hour moving the nectar back and forth from their honey crops, where additional enzymes are added, to their mouths where they 'chew' on it.

Their work as chemists doesn't stop there. They add a second enzyme, glucose oxidase, which further breaks down some of the glucose into gluconic acid and hydrogen peroxide. It is this second chemical reaction which gives honey its antimicrobial properties, as the gluconic acid and hydrogen peroxide make honey inhospitable to bacteria, moulds and fungi. This enzymatic process creates a substance that is both more digestible for the bees and less likely to be attacked by microbes while stored within honeycomb (Collison, 2003). Brilliant!

After all this chemistry of breaking down sugars, the process of honey making is only partially completed. As the story continues, it illustrates more of the magnificence of honey bees. After processing the nectar with enzymes, small droplets of the inverted nectar are deposited on the upper side of honeycomb cell walls where they evaporate the remaining water content. While the collaboration is remarkable between older and younger worker bees sharing the responsibilities of foraging, inverting and storing nectar, the coordination involved in the process of evaporating the nectar from 80 per cent to 17–18 per cent moisture is truly astonishing.

To evaporate moisture, hive bees divide into groups and beat their wings in a coordinated effort to circulate the air within the hive. Some bees fan fresh air into the hive, while others fan moist air out of the hive. They work so beautifully together that they actually create an airflow. As they fan the ripening honey in the comb, they create a hum that emanates from their hive: the sound of their single assembly of individuals in one amalgamated organism.

Along with fanning, hive bees are reducing the water content by externally manipulating nectar in their mouthparts; they form a large drop between their proboscis and their mandibles, exposing the nectar to the air. Also accelerating the evaporation process is the warm temperature of the hive. As bees digest minute amounts of honey, they generate heat. This heat, created by their own metabolism, keeps the temperature of their hive between 92° and 95°F. This warm air is able to draw out and contain the moisture evaporating from the honey.

Inexplicably, the bees know without the aid of any laboratory equipment when the honey has the perfect moisture content and is ready to be capped. Hive bees now cap the cells with a thin layer of beeswax, sealing the final produce into the honeycomb for later consumption.

The great undertaking of transforming nectar into honey is necessary. It would not suffice for honey bees simply to bring back the nectar and place it in the honeycomb. Nectar left in its natural state would ferment and therefore could not be stored as a food source. Also, by converting nectar into honey, they transform it into a far more efficient source of energy. While most flower nectars are a diluted sugary solution, honey is a super-saturated, high-energy carbohydrate. It is an extraordinarily efficient food, providing much greater energy than pure nectar.

Now the bees feast on this stored honey as they need and in doing so they reveal their profound and inspiring sense of community. Bees rarely dine alone and help themselves to honey. They feed each other even when they are near honey-filled

cells and could easily retrieve food themselves. Workers feed each other, as well as feed the queen and the drones. Eating this precious substance is a community event.

During the winters in colder regions of the world, bees form tight clusters on their honeycomb and feed on the stores of honey as they endure months barren of blossoming flowers. It is the collective work of thousands of bees that enables a colony to produce enough honey to survive the winter. Through diligent, hard work, an individual worker bee only produces a minuscule amount of honey in its lifetime (estimated as one twelfth of a teaspoonful). However, the work of each individual is not insignificant, but exemplifies how they collectively create a life-sustaining bounty.

Honey is much more than a mere source of carbohydrates for a colony: it is the manifest embodiment of the collaboration of 50 to 60 thousand individuals carrying out their individual responsibilities to ensure the survival of the collective. Honey bees harmoniously labour and create for the common good.

The exchange of gifts

The goodness they create by their labours of course extends well beyond their hive to flowering plants themselves. By harvesting the sweet gift offered by flowers, bees not only gift each other a substance that ensures their continuity but give back to the flowers by pollinating them and ensuring their continuity. The story of worker bees making honey is inseparable from the story of flowering plants, for it is their symbiotic relationship that brings

honey into the world. Plants provide the raw material to be transformed into a life-sustaining substance. There is no honey without the floral gifts of nectar. In turn, without bees, pollination would be drastically reduced.

This symbiotic relationship between bees and plants began to evolve more than a hundred million years ago. Plants, being well rooted in the soil, clearly cannot move and thus need to rely on external factors to aid their reproduction, and hence survival. Prior to their engagement with bees and other pollinators, early flowering plants (angiosperms) relied solely on wind for pollination. Millions of years of plants and pollinators co-evolving together created another option: pollination by the insect kingdom.

As plants and pollinators co-evolved, they became interdependent, intertwined and commingled. Insects became dependent on nectar and pollen as life-sustaining nourishment, and plants became dependent on insects and other creatures to transport their pollen. Their bond is inseparable as they are entirely dependent on each other for survival.

To lure pollinators, plants not only developed a sweet nectar, but also adapted their colours, textures, shapes, and odours in relation to the pollinator on which they depend. While some plants evolved certain characteristics to attract various species of bees, others evolved to attract other pollinators such as birds, butterflies, moths, bats, beetles, wasps and flies.

The unique specifics of plants and pollinators link them together as partners in pollination. Honey bees are most attracted to sweetly scented, blue and yellow flowers. Butterflies and birds are linked to odourless flowers with bright colours, while bats and moths are drawn to scented flowers that are white or pale in colour. Not surprisingly, blowflies are coupled with brownish flowers with a rank or rotten odour.

Pollinators ensure the lives of flowering plants, as the flowering plants ensure the lives of pollinators. We in turn benefit greatly from their symbiotic relationships. In their effort to produce honey and provide themselves with sustenance, honey bees are simultaneously providing *us* with *our* sustenance as they pollinate many of our crops.

To produce just one pound of honey, bees visit approximately two million flowers. This is only for one pound for one colony, let alone the millions of colonies worldwide that can produce 200 pounds yearly. The amount of flowers pollinated and miles flown to accomplish such a feat is almost beyond comprehension.

Honey, our environment expressed

As the flowers gift the bees with nectar, so the bees gift us with honey, a substance that actually connects us intimately with a particular landscape. In providing us with honey, bees open our senses and enable us to connect with our environment in a way that we would not be able to do otherwise. The honey bee links us with the apple blossoms, not just the apple, the blossoms of meadows and hillsides, the cover crops of clover, and even the weeds we pull and compost. Every region has its distinctive

characteristics, scents and flavours: the eucalyptus honey of the United States, for instance, tastes different from the eucalyptus honey of Australia.

When we consume honey, we are also experiencing the weather, climatic conditions and specific geographic location that all influence honey. Even within a certain locality, differences in the weather can affect the colour and flavour of honey from one year to the next, rendering each annual harvest unique. Thus bees not only connect us to flowers, but to the environment in which they blossomed. They mediate this connection for us.

There is an astonishing variety of unique artisan honeys from around the world originating from floral sources as diverse as acacia, avocado, sage, sunflower, blackberry or pumpkin. Distinctively flavoured honeys include Scottish heather honey which is slightly bitter, Tasmanian leatherwood honey which is robust with a complex, spicy flavour, and pine honey from Turkey which tastes like molasses. From New Zealand, nodding thistle has a light floral taste, while rata is almost salty. Sourwood honey from the United States has a tangy, sometimes gingery taste. From Greece, wild thyme honey has a herbal, grassy flavour, while the lavender honey from France is very sweet and tastes much like the flower itself.

In addition to these unifloral honeys, there are types of combined honey. Though not as revered by honey connoisseurs, blended honey is a combination of honeys from different nectar sources or regions, which gives a product with less distinctive flavours than artisan honeys. To prevent crystallization it is usually pas-

teurized, and filtered through a very fine mesh under pressure to remove extraneous solids such as pollen grains. Raw honey, which naturally crystallizes, has not been pasteurized and contains pollen and small particles of wax.

In its unblended state, though, honey truly is an expression of a place. It is the metamorphosis of a landscape into an aromatic and flavourful form that we can directly experience. The honey bee is the only insect that makes a food consumed by humans. No other insect gifts us with a substance that allows us to savour the nuances of our earth. Perhaps, through this sweet lure, they are trying to connect us to the grandeur of our natural world, helping us to grow in appreciation and admiration, and enlivening our awe of our planet and its rich diversity.

Medicinal honey

As well as connecting us to a particular place and adding sweetness to our lives, honey promotes health and facilitates healing. Medicinal properties of honey have been recognized by many cultures since prehistoric times. Honey was used in ancient Chinese medicine, Indian Ayurvedic medicine, as well as the Roman pharmacopoeia. Hippocrates, Mohammad, Dioscorides and Aristotle also proposed honey as a remedy for many ailments, including eye disorders, ulcers and diseases of the gut. Many of their ancient insights are still acknowledged and appreciated in modern times (*Bee World*, 1999).

Today, honey is used as a soothing remedy for coughs and sore throats. It is also found in many skincare products, including skin creams, lips balms, cosmetics, shampoos and conditioners. Honey is wonderful for nourishing and moisturizing because, being a natural humectant, it attracts and retains moisture. It is this innate quality that renders honey a superb remedy for dry skin, chapped lips and dull hair.

Though honey has an ability to moisturize our skin, it also dehydrates microorganisms. This inherent biological property partially accounts for honey's antimicrobial nature. Honey's low moisture content (less then 18.6 per cent, as we saw) gives it high osmotic pressure. Due to this pressure, honey can readily absorb moisture from, dry out and kill microscopic organisms that enter it. This property, along with its acidity (pH 3.2–4.5) and glucose oxidase system that produces hydrogen peroxide, prevents honey from hosting bacteria, moulds, fungi and other microbes (Collison, 2003). This renders it a substance with remarkable healing properties and many medicinal applications.[1]

Antibiotic and curative properties of honey have been known for thousands of years. The recent resurgence of the use of honey as an effective medicine might be due to the development of antibiotic-resistant bacteria. Honey, which has been found to be effective in laboratory testing against multi-resistant *Staphylococcus aureus* (MRSA), might have potential as a broad-spectrum, antibacterial agent.

Research has shown that not all honeys are equal in their healing qualities. The antibacterial and therapeutic properties of honey depend strongly on the origin.

Manuka honey from New Zealand has antibacterial properties that far surpass those of other honeys. This honey has been effective in treating fungating wounds as well as ulcers resulting from radiation therapy. Other unifloral honeys with high antibacterial potency are buckwheat, chestnut, cotton and honeydew.

The antimicrobial and antifungal nature of honey provides therapeutic benefits in wound care. Along with its ability to fight a broad spectrum of bacteria, honey is truly remarkable in its ability to stimulate healing in wounds, scrapes and burns. Honey provides a moist healing environment, yet draws moisture from the wound and promotes drainage. It also reduces inflammation, removes malodour, as well as

promoting the removal of unhealthy tissue (debridement) and the regeneration of new skin. Even though this extraordinary substance is rather sticky, honey dressings do not adhere to wound surfaces, so changing bandages is easy (Molan, 1999).

The magnificence of honey goes beyond its antibacterial properties and beneficial attributes in wound care. Rudolf Steiner enlightens us about the healing properties of honey in his 1923 lectures on bees. From his anthroposophical perspective, honey is congealed warmth and light that contains curative attributes that preserve health and vigour. Steiner explains that honey contains formative 'hexagonal forces', which we witness in its tendency to crystallize. Honey therefore is especially beneficial for older people where deforming tendencies can be addressed by the structural forces that it provides. Eaten in the right quantity, honey, he said, is an exceptionally strengthening food.

Honey is so much more than a healthier form of sugar. It is a golden elixir that not only soothes our sore throats but also makes our skin shine, strengthens us with its structuring forces, and defends us against unwanted bacteria.

Honey, a substance to ponder

If we are open to learning from the insect world, what else can bees reveal to us that can be healing? Are they in fact teaching us something by working to convert nectar into honey for the common good of the hive?

By observing them we discover that

bees would not be able to store enough honey for the winter if they were in the business of 'all against all': of getting from each other and the planet rather than giving. It is in helping the flowers propagate that they receive life-sustaining nectar. It is in giving their individually collected nectar to the collective hive that they receive a bounty to survive a winter. They work, communicate and collaborate for the common good.

Are we moved to contemplate, over a teaspoon of this sweet liquid, that there might be something profound to learn from the story of honey making? If we are willing to humble ourselves, might there be ways honey bee behaviour can actually inform our human behaviour? The bees' dire situation is strengthening our environmental awareness, but can their way of living in tune with nature strengthen our sense of environmental stewardship so that we too live in more harmonious balance with our surroundings?

Can the honey bees enlighten us with new insight into our interconnectedness? Can our individual and unique abilities, in our everyday lives and deeds, impact positively on the greater community, the regional and even global 'hive'? Can we as a planet of individuals work together as one organism to sustain ourselves? Can we honour our individual roles while holding a community-based consciousness, knowing that we all play a part in creating our planetary experiences?

What can we co-create together, both to bring more sweetness to our lives and to provide healing to each other? Can we learn that there is no taking without giving? We have brought bees to the very edge of devastation by our greed and lack of harmony with our surroundings. Can they teach us new, less selfish ways to live?

Bibliography

Collison, Clarence H., *What Do You Know?*, A.I. Root Company, Ohio 2003

Molan, Peter C., 'Why honey is effective as a medicine. Its use in modern medicine', *Bee World* 80 (2): 80–92 (1999) Bee Product Science, 23 March 2010

Steiner, Rudolf, *Bees*, Anthroposophic Press, 1998

Note

1. Note, this article presents information about the medicinal aspects of honey, but not medical advice on its use.

GOLDEN THREADS AND THE GOLDEN FLEECE

Johannes Wirz

Imagine the early spring. During recent days, the sun has gained in strength, the snow is melting away and the first willow trees have opened their buds. On his afternoon walk, the attentive rambler hears a gentle humming sound. Above his head, hundreds of honey bees are diligently collecting the first pollen of the year. In the hive, these precious goods are welcome. Since late January, the queen has been laying eggs, and the whole colony has taken great care in raising the brood, warming and feeding it. Pollen is urgently needed.

Some seven months later the first clear, frosty October nights announce the approach of winter. Leaf mustard sown for green manure has resisted the cold, and colours the shortening days with its yellow hue. The cold has devastated most insect life. Migrating butterflies like the monarch have headed south long ago, others like the small tortoiseshell have found their hide-aways under stacks of wood, in quiet barns or pavement cracks, to sleep their long winter sleep; and yet others like the marbled white have secured the existence of their descendants by depositing eggs, larvae or pupae for hibernation.

But in the absence of other pollinating insects, the honey bees are still around. By their hundreds and thousands they take advantage of the remaining sunny afternoons before the long weeks of winter to come, collecting the last drops of nectar and grains of pollen to replenish stores for their future sisters: the brood to be reared after the winter.

Both situations display the specific characteristics of the honey bee. Whatever the season, they are present in great numbers to pollinate the flowers, so that seeds can mature and fruits ripen. With an unsurpassed fidelity and precision, they ensure that the styles of one flower species are pollinated with only the correct grains of pollen. What is so clearly visible at the beginning and at the end of the flowering season holds true throughout the year. Honey bees engage with the abundance of flora around their hives and transform it into a cornucopia of life in relation to both plants and hives.

If we think of the honey bees as the orchestra in the symphony of the pollinators, then solitary bees and butterflies represent the soloists in different ways. Solitary bees have a short and exclusive performance on the stage of flowers: some three to six short weeks. It is an enigma how they always manage to appear just at the right moment, when 'their' flowers start to bloom. And they will pass away as soon as their only source of pollen has withered. Unlike the honey bees, which build a whole camp for their progeny, solitary bees prepare rooms with single cradles in the hollow stems of plants, or narrow tunnels,

built in sand or clay, each one furnished with just the right amount of pollen to secure the development of the larva hatching from the egg to the pupa stage. For many months the siblings remain enclosed – either awake or dormant, who can tell? The next year – as if by magic – they manage to leave their nursery in the *opposite* order from egg deposition. The bee from the last-laid egg leaves the pupa and the shelter first, while the one from the first egg politely waits and emerges last. How this is possible still remains their secret.

Of course the solitary bees from spring are not kindred with those in summer, and those of the summer will never meet with those of early autumn; and not a single solitary bee has ever seen her mother. By contrast, honey bees from one colony know their mother intimately and spend most of their time in the circle of their sisters. However, they share with the solitary bee the unique faculty of pollination fidelity.

In common with many other insects, including butterflies, beetles and flies, honey bees have the capacity to visit many different flowers. But what a difference! Butterflies, and flies even more so, like to swap haphazardly from one plant species to another, often guided by colours rather than by the species' specific odour or taste. Shorter or longer visits to flowers are interrupted by phases of egg deposition. Though mist and wind may carry them long distances away, they do not long for a home. Or to put it another way, 'home' is wherever they are. Honey bees, by contrast, return home every day with the same fidelity as that with which they secure the

right pollen on the right style. At the same time they share the butterflies' flexibility of flower choice, but of course with an important proviso. For a given period of time they stick to one species. No wonder that the pollen deposited artistically on their hind legs is stored with the same fidelity in the combs; you will never find a mixture of colours. Instead, cells of different colours are arranged fancifully as on a palette – yellow, red, black-blue, orange or pink.

The same holds true for honey. Some beekeepers take advantage of this fact and move their bees around to collect honey from orchards, acacia, oil-seed rape, chestnut trees, or sunflower crops, following the blooming with their colonies. Those who cannot or do not want to move the bees unwittingly collect a blend, because in the course of honey extraction the nicely separated honeys mix.

Spinning threads in the landscape

One kilo of honey requires some two million visits to flowers. If all these flowers were just 10 cm apart from each other, the distance covered to produce one jar of honey would account for some 200 kilometres. Of course, this calculation can be extended. Assuming that one colony must collect some 120 kilos of honey to survive through the year, the distance they travel comes to around 24,000 kilometres. Less conservative estimates would increase the distance accordingly. Since there are some 2.5 million colonies in the United States, the distance covered is likely to exceed 50

billion kilometres! Given the average distance of the sun from the earth of 150 million kilometres, these calculations give an impression of the extraordinary labours of the honey bees, year on year. But behind these numbers lies more: the mystery of the encounter between flowers and pollinators, as a story of harmonious mutual benefit.

Let us start to observe the apiary on a sunny summer day, standing behind a hive. Bees leave and arrive continuously. Others, distinguishable by the bright colour on the dorsal side of the thorax, are dancing rhythmically with vertical movements, heads facing the hive and the entrance hole. Closer inspection shows that the pale colour of these bees is the effect of many tiny bristles – these are young bees on the cusp of becoming foragers, who first must learn to identify the site and the hive.

The leaving and arriving bees exhibit different modes of flight. Bees take off with an incredible energy and speed. Almost all the time one can observe that they depart in a number of discrete, different directions. There must be more than one location of a good nectar source. Or to put it another way, colonies like to forage on a diversity of plant species. We know that collecting bees recruit sisters by the waggle dance, an intriguing movement that indicates the direction, distance and quality of the nectar source. Returning bees are slower: their flight sometimes looks insecure, and often they have difficulty in landing properly on the entrance board. Whoever has carried a big backpack on top of a mountain will understand why. Either their stomachs are filled with nectar or their hindlegs are heavily loaded with pollen. Their direction home is less coordinated, and their return paths show a continuum of different angles.

Most of the time we do not know where they are returning from or heading to, with two exceptions: in the case of honey robbery within the same apiary, or in summer, when there is a solitary linden tree in full blossom, in a landscape otherwise empty of flowers. In this situation, you can trace the path of the bees as they fly to the tree, and you may smell the typical odour of linden nectar and pollen wafting through the entrance hole from the inside of the hive.

After this first impression, let us walk into our garden. Poppies are flowering and raspberries have opened their blossoms. Different modes of foraging behaviour by the bees can be observed with the two plant species. In the poppies they seem to take a hasty bath in the receptacle, eager to switch to the next flower, which sure enough will be poppy again. They are collecting pollen, the colour of which is almost black, and they do not appear disturbed by the presence of other bees and insects. In the small and colourless flowers of the raspberries the scenario is different. Bees sit on the convex flower, head down, and the attentive observer may see that they hunt for nectar with the proboscis extended. The duration of a visit to one blossom is long, and the frequency of switching to the next flower is low. Here, the foraging bee is aggressive towards uninvited guests; she wants to be alone. The two activities are reminiscent of the rhythms of a quick beat and a slow drum.

In both cases, the path of a single bee from flower to flower is a kind of random flight, the best option for guaranteeing that all flowers are visited by different pollinators. In addition, every visit is governed by a kind of delicate analysis: the availability and quality of pollen and nectar is quickly checked – in the case of poor quantity or quality the flower is swiftly abandoned and the next one is tried. If we were to trace the journeys of these foraging bees, we would realize that every single one is spinning a continuous thread from the hive to the flowers and back to the hive. Continuity and randomness, necessity and chance, are the features which secure the thorough and complete success of pollination – but also a rich and tasty feed for all the present and future sisters in the hive.

The golden fleece

In the light of the early morning sun, little imagination is needed to see flying bees as golden sparks, and it is not very difficult to picture the forager bees laying golden threads across the flower meadow or the blossoming fruit tree. With a little more effort we could reintegrate all these threads into a single whole. All the bees weave a fabric together in a joint and concerted action: a tapestry or, to be more mythological, the golden fleece. They 'wrap' trees, shrubs, meadows and landscapes in the threads of their activity. The size of the stitches varies in relation to the abundance of the flowers. They are narrow in blooming fruit trees, and wide on sparsely distributed flowers in a meadow. This is in some ways reminiscent of the work by wrapping artists Christo and Jeanne Claude, pictures of which – such as the covered Reichstag in Berlin – have made their way around the world.

Beside the honey bees, which in a certain way create the underlying fabric of this golden fleece, all the other pollinators – fewer in number and in a shorter time – also add their threads. Butterflies, beetles, solitary bees and flies add shorter or longer fibres to the whole weft. The common blue butterfly puts in narrow stitches, carefully woven between the blossoms of its nectar plant, the lotus. Its piece of art does not exceed a few square metres, the area sufficient to sustain an entire small population. The majestic swallowtail, in contrast, adds mesh of gigantic size. After a short visit to a flower, it may fly for 100 metres or more before it comes to rest again. The six-spot burnet makes tiny delicate stitches in the fleece, sitting for hours or sometimes even days on the very same flower of a field scabious.

Unlike the wrapped trees of Christo and Claude, the imagination of the golden fleece depends on our own inner visualizing capacity. The golden fleece is an inner experience, ephemeral and only present as long as you create it yourself – lost if you lack the power or time to create it. At the same time, whenever you can recall it, it is a certain and vivid experience throughout the year, from spring, through summer and autumn to winter. Every time you create the fleece in your imagination, you realize an indisputable truth – the spiritual reality of the action of the honey bees and their pollinating partners!

The ensoulment of landscape

What substance is the golden fabric made of? Or put in another way: what kind of essence is woven from flower to flower by all these pollinators? It is soul substance, or as Rudolf Steiner puts it, 'astral substance' – meaning both that it originates from the stars, and manifests through the innate wisdom at work in creatures. What insects weave around the earth is, from a certain perspective, the most fundamental contribution to the evolution of our planet, of all plants, and of human beings themselves. This was known in older times when people were still familiar with the 'scala naturae'. In this view, rocks, water, air and warmth – the four elements of ancient Greece – provided the foundation for all other beings. Plants were considered to be the purest and most immediate manifestation of life, providing the basis for all the sentient beings, the animals, with their irreducible qualities of soul. What is the task of the human being in this picture? According to many natural philosophers he is able and obliged to bring nature to self-awareness – that is, to see, feel and think of her beauty, and to praise her through scientific ideas and laws, through monuments, sculptures and paintings in the arts, and through agriculture as much as through the erecting of cathedrals; and last but not least, through religious and spiritual imaginations in which nature's essential being is truly grasped.

The golden fleece is the ensoulment of landscape by pollinating insects. Its wonderful, distinctive harmony is easily apparent: pollination (alongside the harvest of propolis, an invaluable substance for the health of honey bees[1]) is the only process in which creatures *give* something to plants by *taking* something from them. Think of grazing cows in contrast to foraging honey bees. This 'taking' creates vibrant abundance. Flowers and plants are separate and cannot move towards one another. Without pollinators most of the vegetative life forms would be condemned to perish. Most annual flowering plants survive by pollination, exclusively. Therefore, the golden fleece is not merely a fanciful idea, but a reality that must be woven unceasingly year after year.

The wonder of the co-evolution of flowering plants and pollinators is the scientific expression of this fact. The interdependence goes further. A plethora of birds rely on seeds and insects, and in consequence birds of prey cannot exist without them. Without the pollinators therefore, we would lose not only magic for our eyes, but also for our ears – the world would become a sad and silent place indeed. The lesson is an easy one to learn: the ecology, beauty and diversity of nature lives and evolves on the basis of mutual giving and taking.

This thought is intensified by another, seemingly disturbing truth. Pollination triggers processes of both maturation and decay. In forming seeds the mother plants must fade away to secure the future of their offspring. The German poet and thinker Johann Wolfgang von Goethe wrote, serenely: 'Life is nature's most beautiful invention; and death her brilliant trick for having ever more life.' If this is correct, then withering and death are also a kind of art. Without ripening, ageing and death we would lack fruit, berries, and vegetables –

for food, as well as for beauty. We would lack the golden grass, the golden fields of barleycorn, wheat, rye or oats – the most impressive and touching pictures of maturation and decay, albeit independent of pollinating insects.

Coming back to the honey bees, they help to close the circle of everlasting life. Without their golden fleece there could be no end and therefore no new beginning, no rhythmic pulse between burgeoning life, maturation and withering. The great holes in the fabric caused by the unexpected death of whole bee colonies – sometimes inevitable, but more often provoked by human beings – must be mended as rapidly as possible to ensure that the beauty and truth of nature can go on perpetuating itself.

Note

1. See the article by David Heaf, pp. 64–65.

DRONES: THE HOLIEST OF BEES

Jacqueline Freeman

Drones (male bees) make up about one per cent of the hive's population, usually a few hundred per hive. Female worker bees make up the other 99 per cent of the hive and handle all the hive tasks — gathering pollen and nectar, hive cleaning, comb building, feeding the queen and the baby bees, and hive protection. In conventional beekeeping, drones are presumed to be needed for one thing only, mating with a virgin queen.

In conventional beekeeping, queens are artificially bred and not impregnated in the wild. Most beekeepers believe drones simply take up space, eating honey which could be better used by the worker bees or harvested by the beekeeper. Following this belief about the drones' lack of usefulness, most conventional and even organic bee-keepers cull out drone eggs, leaving only worker bees and a queen.

Interestingly enough, no matter how many times beekeepers find and kill the drones, the queen continually lays more drone brood to replace the missing drones. Beekeepers think they're helping the hive but the hive obviously doesn't feel that way. The hive wants drones.

Drones look different from the female worker bees. They have enormous eyes, a large stinger-less body, and a more leisurely pace than the workers. Rudolf Steiner called drones 'the sense organ of the hive' and said they are responsible for reflecting back to the hive the feeling states in which the hive dwells. When I asked about the role of the drones,[1] the bees said . . .

The drones sacrifice themselves. They are the holiest of beings. They make the prayer sound within the hive and are not distracted by tasks. They sing and their sound fills us with love. They make a round sound that surrounds us with prayer. They sing for the brood, sing for the birth. Their sound pulls the brood as they are being born through the light of Creation.

Drones are exquisitely conscious of the sense impressions within the hive, fully in connection with the historical context within which bees dwell. Like Aboriginal and African cultures who sing ceremonial songs to birth babies into life, the drones sing their Creation Song to transmit knowledge of the bees' role in the world. Drones convey bee culture to the next generation through their song.

The drones' song imprints the developing, 'unborn' bees with the vibration of Creation. The sound moves through the hive like a prayer, becoming part of the vibratory being of each bee. As the bees mature, they come to embody information that is later passed on to the flowers during pollination.

There is another clue that hints at the unique role played by drones: their ability to visit other hives. Each hive has its own

distinct scent that comes from the queen's pheromone. All bees in that hive carry her scent on them. So if a worker bee from a robber hive goes a-wandering to see what's inside the hive down the lane, the second hive's guard bees know immediately that she is not from their hive and they'll chase her off.

Worker bees in a strong hive sometimes try to enter other hives to find out if they can steal the other hive's honey and enlarge their own larders. The robber bees test the second hive's guard bees to see how secure their front door is. If it's weak, they'll gather up an invading force to steal the other hive's honey. For this reason, all guard bees defend their entrances and don't allow intruders from other hives inside.

Unlike worker bees, drones can visit any hive. They land at the entrance, stroll past the guard bees and head inside. The guard bees step aside and let them in even though they know the drones are from another hive. Why would they do that and where are the drones going?

Common sense would say that the one place you wouldn't want strangers to go in your home would be in the nursery where all the babies are, but that's exactly where the drones go! The drones go directly into the brood area where the eggs and newborns are. Seemingly 'selflessly', they join the other drones for two tasks, to provide warmth to the brood and to sing the celebratory birth song.

The baby larvae are surrounded by the hive's song, a vibratory lullaby that permeates the eggs in their cells. As the brood grow in their cells, they hear the drones singing the song of the world, of the past and future of the hive. The drone song imparts to them volumes of information about the spiritual and functional purpose of honey bees.

The song is knowledge. The song tells about a world with the sky and the earth and a horizon between, the scent of the wind. Drones sing the Creation song to pattern the birth door. During gestation they encode each larva with the knowledge of 'how to bee', overlaid with cosmic knowledge that blueprints how the world comes into being each day and how the hive helps carry the world into the future. When the larvae are sufficiently mature, the creation song calls them out of the cell and stimulates the sensory organs of the baby bee. The linkup is an invitation and an answer, a call and response as they leave the cell.

The sound in which the brood are immersed invokes hexagonal quality even as they are being formed inside one. This quality, as they grow, will come to have great meaning to them.

The drones' Creation Song involves elaborately precise vibrational communication about the organization of minerals, and a map of the relationship of the mineral forces contained in pollen. Pollen is depicted as a vast compendium of mineral knowledge. This chemical language reveals the right relationship between the minerals, with a specific awareness of silica.

Simultaneously they also are imbued with a sense impression of the worker bees' practical tasks through the constant hum and vibration within the hive. The movement of the comb and the individual tasks occurring upon it are conveyed to all bees in the hive through vibration. In the workers' hum, the brood bees hear and understand the industry of the worker bees in their daily tasks.

During their pre- and post-emergence states, the new bees hear a combined harmony of two songs:

> *From the worker bees we hear,*
> *'Come and join the work,'*
> *and from the drones,*
> *'Come and join the world.'*

Bees need to know the changing tasks they will take up in and out of the hive. They also have to know their larger purpose, the bees' role in the world. The workers' hum tells the bees what they will do once they are born. The drone song tells them why they will do that. The combined sound has a sense of celebration about it that sparks the linkup in the newly emerging baby bees and brings happiness to all.

The drones are the only bees who sing the Creation Song that instils in the new bees all this knowledge. The brood bees emerge with an inherent knowing. If new bees don't hear the drone song and don't learn this language because the beekeeper has got rid of the drones, bees are less able to fulfil their role in the fields and on earth.

Drones need to be there to convey to the hive's future foragers the intelligence they will carry out to the fields and bring to the flowers. In a robustly healthy hive, each bee resonates with the Creation Song. Drones need to be there in the hive so they can bring forth the balanced sound vigorous hives make, the sound of healthy, exuberantly alive hives.

The drones, bless them, sing a song of expressive gratitude, a prayer of full connection with Creation.

Note

1. The author is able to perceive nature intelligences, particularly the honey bees, clairvoyantly.

PRESERVING THE INTEGRITY OF THE SUPER-ORGANISM: INDIVIDUAL AND SOCIAL IMMUNITY

David Heaf

One of the most pleasurable moments in beekeeping is when the crown board or inner cover is lifted off the hive and a stream of warm, moist, fragrant air wafts up into one's face. The scent is indefinable, sweetly resinous perhaps, yet instantly recognizable as that of a bee colony. That simple act of exposing the bees to the open air, a normal routine in modern beekeeping, can happen to a single hive dozens of times in a season. But what does it cost the bees in trips to fetch nectar to replace the lost energy and restore the lost warmth of the hive?

When we open a hive, however briefly, we perturb or even violate the integrity of the super-organism within. Of course, bees are immensely adaptable and can survive surprising challenges. For example a colony can winter alfresco in a temperate climate in the branches of a tree. Many colonies have survived their hives being toppled and left open for days. Yet any disturbance of the integrity of their shelter comes at some cost to the bees. We will discuss here how a colony achieves its integrity and suggest ways in which we beekeepers can help.

Considering the organisms of the living world from the simplest to the most complex, we notice that not only does the complexity of the species increase, but also the degree of autonomy, or emancipation, from some of the influences of the environment. The bee, somewhere intermediate in this continuum, separates itself from its environment at two levels. The individual bee is enclosed in a hard exoskeleton, and, being a social insect, the society of bees seeks to enclose itself within a protective covering.

A newly emerged swarm, after clustering around its queen, usually quite close to the nest whence it issued, prioritizes finding a cavity to shelter in. Scouts survey the local options, often revisiting cavities found before the swarm issued. They are choosy, preferring cavities of about 40 litres to those of say 10 or 100 litres. After a complex interaction between the scouts at the potential nest sites, and between the scouts and the rest of the swarm, a quorum is reached in favour of one cavity, and the swarm, guided by the scouts, flies to its new home.

Inside it the bees gain a second layer of protection from the environment. The integrity of the super-organism is obviously better assured with a sheath round it to keep out the wind, rain, hail and snow. In nature the shelter is commonly the wood of a hollow tree. Dissections of bee nests show that the thickness of the protection afforded by trees averages about 15 cm.

This is a major contribution to the bees' efforts to maintain thermal homeostasis, an even temperature, especially in comparison with modern beehives, which usually have walls only three-quarters of an inch thick. For much of the year in many climates, the ambient temperature is below that essential for the healthy life of the colony, i.e. about 35°C. Thicker walls cut heat escape by this route. Furthermore, trees usually provide an additional enhancement of the colony's autonomy. Whereas the thick trunk helps insulate from the cold, shading by the canopy of leaves protects from solar radiation. Achieving such shading in an apiary is not always possible, so hives are sometimes given roofs that form a solar shield over a ventilated space.

Returning to our newly housed bees: the cluster gradually flows upwards to the top of the cavity and hangs there while some bees start comb building using the nectar and honey they travelled with. First one comb begins, then another next to and parallel to it, and so on. All are fixed to the top of the cavity and all are about two bee thicknesses apart. Warmth is very important in the construction, for at a certain point it must be heated above normal nest temperature so that the wax flows into the familiar hexagonal pattern that uses the least amount of material to give the greatest strength and storage capacity.

The combs eventually span the diameter of the cavity and the bees fix the edges of the comb to the walls, leaving peripheral galleries for access between each comb.

The overall form comprises a series of parallel spaces, or seams, closed at the top, in which the cluster continues its activities.

This arrangement effectively retains the precious warmth of the colony. The bees regulate it only through the seam openings at the bottoms of the combs where gaseous exchange and humidity regulation also take place, either passively by diffusion or actively by the bees fanning their wings. The fixing of the comb to the ceiling and walls, apart from the interruptions in the relatively small area of peripheral galleries, means that there is little opportunity for convection currents to carry heat rapidly from the warm atmosphere of the seams of bees to the nest's cold walls.

We can contrast this with the situation in a modern frame hive. Frame beekeeping achieved practicability when the Revd L.L. Langstroth recognized the need for a 'bee space' of about 8 mm between the frames and the hive walls, because without it the bees stick the frames firmly in place. His bee space is often represented as a discovery, although it is more an invention for the convenience of beekeepers, as nothing like it exists in a natural nest. Even the galleries, about a bee space in width, are not the same, because in frame hives the bees often recreate them between the combs and the frame woodwork. Frames, with their peripheral bee space, create a draughty alleyway round the comb sides and tops where air currents can carry the heat away from the nest. But hives that effectively retain the nest warmth have long existed, such as skeps and horizontal and vertical top-bar hives. Because these lack frames, they are less convenient for beekeepers. Even the *Einraumbeute* or one-box hive, though a frame hive, tends towards retaining nest heat by virtue of its cloth covering over the top-bars.

We should not overlook that thermal homeostasis also means being able to keep cool in hot weather. In housing themselves in a hollow tree cavity the bees have gained only a certain amount of autonomy vis-à-vis environmental influences. They can readily generate heat by muscle action fuelled by honey, but what if it gets too hot? Their main connection with the surroundings is now via one or more cavity entrances. Here must take place the exchange of gases for respiration as well as the removal of excess heat and moisture. This is often accelerated by coordinated wing fanning by workers. In addition to cavity volume, there is evidence that bees actually choose their entrance size, such is the advanced state of their autonomy, preferring entrances of 10–20 cm^2. This relatively small aperture plays another important part in the autonomy of the super-organism as an easily defensible gateway against intruders, including carnivorous insects such as wasps and hornets as well as robber bees from other colonies. If the bees find the aperture too big they reduce it with propolis, of which more later. We can view this as the first line in the colony's immune protection – discriminating 'self' from 'not self'.

Entrance ventilation is often particularly noticeable on windless evenings after productive nectar foraging. Hives sound like extractor fans. If you put your face level with the entrance hole, that wonderful aroma I mentioned can again be sampled, this time dominated by flower scents and heavily laden with moisture as the bees dry off the nectar to produce honey. The whole apiary is filled with an almost overpowering scent.

The immune system of higher animals, something that protects their integrity from foreign organisms and thus maintains health, has its analogy in honey bees at two levels. One is the immune system as it is generally conceived, a molecular and cellular recognition system that can detect when something that is not 'self', i.e. in this case what is not bee, has entered the body, and can destroy it. In the individual bee, when the cuticle, the barrier between self and the outside world has been breached and the invader has survived other chemical defenses such as an acid environment, this immunity occurs via recognition proteins analogous to antibodies in higher animals, and through cells of the haemolymph, the bee's 'blood', that engulf invading pathogens such as bacteria. The other is what is commonly referred to as social immunity, a property of the colony super-organism. Although there is little the beekeeper can do to enhance the immune system of the individual bee apart from ensuring that colonies have access to plentiful and diverse flora without excessive competition from other bees, social immunity can easily be impaired by beekeepers.

Essential to social immunity, though infuriating to frame beekeepers, is a brown or orange sticky substance prepared by the bees called propolis. A clue to its role is its name meaning 'before the city'. It is a combination of the complex resinous exudates of plants and various proportions of beeswax, depending on what the bees want it for. As their 'medical chest', or better still, 'herbal remedy', it is a first line of defense against pathogens – bacterial and fungal – for the whole colony (the city). It is coated on the inside of the nest cavity and on the honeycombs. It fills cracks, stops draughts, waterproofs and even entombs invading hive beetles or embalms mice that have got in and been killed, but are too heavy for the bees to drag out. Propolis even smells like an antiseptic, and certainly tastes so if a lump is chewed to stop a sore throat in its tracks. Recently beekeepers have been encouraged to allow a good propolis envelope to build up inside their hives. This means both avoiding scraping it off hiveware at every opportunity and con-sidering leaving the inside walls of hives with a rough-sawn finish, because bees generally do not propolize smoothly planed walls. Its importance to the colony as an additional 'skin' to maintain integrity is illustrated by the fact that, in an expanding nest, the bees do not apply propolis indiscriminately to the whole cavity, but only to the region next to the combs. Also, when the nurse bees scrupu-lously clean out the comb cells they line them with a thin coating of propolis. The cleaned cells appear to have brightly polished floors indicating that the queen is on a new round of egg laying.

But of course, despite the protective shell, parasites do get into the nest and pose a challenge to a colony's integrity from within. The most troublesome in large parts of the world is the ectoparasite *Varroa destructor*. Bees groom themselves and each other to remove it, sometimes disabling the mite by biting. Several minutes can pass before the mite is dis-lodged. As *V. destructor* also feeds on the young bees it is not surprising that bees have developed an ability to detect mite activity in the brood, uncap the cells and

remove damaged pupae. This hygienic behaviour also applies to brood diseases caused by bacteria and fungi, such as foul brood and chalk brood. Furthermore, pathogens and even *V. destructor* are sus-ceptible to deliberate raising of the brood nest temperature by the bees. This is analogous to the curative effect of fever in higher animals. Conversely bees that have been reared at sub-optimal temperatures are more susceptible to tracheal mites and several diseases associated with micro-organism pathogens, for example chalk brood and foul brood, are more likely to occur if the brood is cooled. Indeed it is chilling, not overheating, that is most fre-quently associated with health impair-ment. Optimum warmth contributes significantly to preserving the super-organism's integrity, so it is vital to design and manage hives to retain warmth in cold conditions.

Two other behaviours help control dis-ease: one is that undertaker bees remove the corpses of any bees that happen to die at home. It is marvellous to watch them struggling to drag a corpse from the entrance and launch themselves into the air, trying to get the corpse as far away from the hive as possible, and often crash landing only a foot or so away. The other behaviour is the intricate division of labour whereby different tasks fall to different age groups of bees. Older bees are more prone to spread disease in the nest. But in foraging they literally fly themselves to death. If they die away from the hive, as is normally the case, they take the disease with them.

A little-researched area in apiology, though one that could improve understanding of bee super-organism integrity, is the role of non-pathogenic microorganisms. Several bacilli, moulds and fungi have already been identified in feral and hived colonies, and there are likely to be many more. Lactic acid bacteria, present in the bee gut, are known to inhibit the growth of the organisms responsible for foul brood and chalk brood. Whether this is a significant factor in the living colony remains to be seen. However, we do know that these bacteria are involved in the preparation of bee bread, a fermentation product of pollen and honey. As bee bread is fed to the bee larvae, they may be taking medicine as they eat.

It often surprises beekeepers to hear mention of retention of scent in the nest; heat retention is immediately understood, but not scent retention. The Austrian beekeeper Johannes Thür introduced this concept. I have long puzzled over it. He regarded it as essential for a germ-free atmosphere. Thus, if it can be substantiated, it is clearly something to do with maintaining the integrity of the super-organism. A preliminary indication that he may be right is that the nest atmosphere contains two volatile fatty acids, acetic acid and formic acid. Both have antiseptic properties. Indeed, acetic acid's food-preserving function is well known. It is also not improbable that volatiles released from the plant resins in propolis may contribute to the 'germ-free atmosphere'. This could be part of the resinous aroma that greets the beekeeper on removing the hive covering.

Another aspect of retention of nest scent, to which Thür did not allude, probably because it was hardly known in his time, is the bouquet of pheromones. These volatile chemical messengers, acting like external hormones, are highly important for colony communication and thus for both organization and integrity. Pheromones chemically characterized, together with those postulated from observed behaviours, number in dozens. Each brings its own message. For example, the queen's mandibular pheromone complex powerfully influences worker behaviour. Remove the queen for only minutes, and workers scurry all over the hive while scouts comb the surroundings. It is not easy for humans to smell these scents — although Nasonov pheromone, released when bees fan to guide nest mates home, is faintly lemony — but bees are highly sensitive to them. As pheromone function differs, and their mixtures subtly change their message according to dosage, combination, context, synergy and whether primer pheromones have taken effect, the subject of bee chemical communication is proving richer than previously dreamed. The pheromone picture has a spatial and temporal distribution. Indeed, we can talk of the 'pheromonal structure' of a bee colony, which like the whole colony has its own integrity. What happens to this integrity when the hive is not only opened, letting out the heat and scent, but also has its furniture rearranged as the beekeeper shuffles framed combs, perhaps removing some and adding others from another hive? How quickly does the colony undo the damage? What resources does this consume and what does it cost in bee journeys to replace them?

Another important structural aspect of the super-organism is its thermal structure. Thermal imaging studies by Juergen Tautz's group at the University of Würzburg vividly illustrate it. The brood nest is not just a uniformly warm space; the heat also has a spatial distribution. Empty cells in brood combs, formerly regarded as resulting from aberrations in the queen's laying or diseased larvae, now appear to be for 'heater' bees to enter and warm surrounding pupae. It has also been found that differential heating of brood results in different behaviours in the resulting adults. Thus whilst it is acknowledged, even by beekeepers, that overall chilling of the brood can increase proneness to disease, impair physical development and even learning and memory of bees, disrupting the thermal structure could have subtler influences as regards programming the division of labour in the colony, and thus its fitness. This is evidenced by the fact that bees raised at different temperatures in the normal range from 32–36°C show differences in their task assignments when adults.

Comb, obviously a vital part of the bee super-organism and certainly more than just its skeleton, seems relatively little studied as regards its optimal qualities for maximizing the health of the colony. Modern beekeepers give bees sheets of recycled beeswax foundation embossed with the hexagonal pattern of the bases of the comb's cells. In the resulting comb, the foundation forms the middle wall or midrib which is significantly thicker and thus less pliable than in natural comb. Furthermore, foundation cell sizes are a *uniform* worker-cell size, even though natural comb shows a *range* of cell sizes. Obviously cells for the larger drones are much bigger, but there is a subtler differentiation amongst worker brood cells too. Restricting a colony to worker foundation limits the space available for making drone comb, risking suppressing drone-brood rearing below a healthy proportion of the total. Just how important drones are is made clear in Jacqueline Freeman's article (pp. 55–58).

Another problem with industrial foundation is that it contains a cocktail of insecticides, some of which beekeepers have used against mites in the hives from which the beeswax was obtained. To get round this problem, some organic beekeepers make their own foundation or even run foundationless hives.

An advantage of going foundationless is that the wall thickness and cell-size range better correspond to the natural situation. Different cell sizes result in various-sized adult workers. The bee's body size can affect task performance, e.g. foraging distance, but it is not clear if body-size diversity is essential in a healthy colony. Many organic beekeepers hold that cell sizes smaller than those used in industrial foundation are more natural and help bees combat mites. Indeed, 'small-cell' advo-

cates claim to manage entirely without miticides. However, several short-term studies by apiologists have failed to show any beneficial effect of reducing cell size, whether against *V. destructor* or tracheal mites. To resolve these conflicting findings, there is clearly scope for further experimentation.

Natural comb hives, such as skeps, are relatively rare nowadays, especially in industrialized countries. However, many beekeepers use top-bar hives which achieve comb that is near to natural, the only constraint placed on it being the distance between the midribs, which is predetermined by beeswax starter-strips. Research has yet to determine if natural or near-natural comb is better for superorganism integrity than comb built on foundation in frames. However, in view of the functions of comb — support for the brood and food stores, and indeed the entire colony, insulation in winter, an acoustic communication system, a retainer of pheromone markings (memory) and a dance floor for the waggle dance — it would be surprising if some crucial differences between natural and artificial did not emerge. An indication that bees are not entirely happy with foundation comb is that they chew away the bottom and edge attachments to the frames so that the comb hangs freely enough to resonate properly during acoustic communication.

The foregoing shows that there is frequently a conflict between the intentions of bees and those of beekeepers. Indeed, any hive design tends to be a compromise between the needs of both. Housing for bees can range from purely natural to industrially artificial. Increasing artificiali-

zation can be listed somewhat as follows, each step being an intensification of the treatments we impose on our bees:

1. Putting bees in a container (e.g. skep, hollow log)
2. Providing top-bars with comb guides (e.g. Kenyan & Warré hives)
3. Providing frames
4. Providing frames with foundation
5. Providing a mesh floor
6. Nadiring/Supering (adding new boxes below/above)
7. Hive opening
8. Moving hives
9. Feeding (e.g. planting forage, feeding honey)
10. Removing honey
11. Controlling swarming
12. Suppressing drones
13. Brood-nest spreading
14. Providing a queen excluder
15. Emergency sugar feeding
16. Artificial queen breeding
17. Transhumance
18. Removing too much honey and substituting sugar syrup
19. Medicating with so-called organic treatments (e.g. powdered sugar, organic acids present in the hive, essential oils present in the hive)
20. Medicating with synthetic pyrethroids and/or antibiotics

This list could be drafted as a matrix showing branching points according to the choice of hive. Many of the practices listed are addressed by other contributors to this book. I would like to conclude by concentrating just on medication.

Encouraged by apiologists in the USA, Scandinavia and France reporting long-term survival of unmedicated colonies challenged by varroa, when I started my experiment with Warré hives – vertical top-bar hives using near-natural comb – I dispensed entirely with medication. I continued medicating (thymol and oxalic acid) my frame hives until 1 January 2009. Now all my bees are exposed to the full ravages of varroa, and indeed natural selection. I see this as the only sustainable way for the future of beekeeping. Either that or we will continue to eternity on the treadmill of putting chemicals in our hives. My objections to using chemicals are not so much the cost or the inconvenience but what they do to the bees and honey. From the outset I steered clear of synthetic pyrethroids as I realized that they were already becoming ineffective in my locality because varroa was becoming tolerant to them. But even the so-called 'soft' organic treatments, which, as a novice beekeeper I was told were essential to colony survival, are poisonous to the bees and could also finish up in the honey. One only has to catch a whiff of the commonly used formic acid to realize what the bees must have to endure when it is vaporized at them in unnaturally high concentrations. The toxic effect of organic acids on bees and queens is already well documented. When crystals of thymol, a compound originally from the essential oils of thyme, but now synthesized industrially, is placed in the hive, the workers do their best to get rid of it as fast as possible. The unpleasant smell is clearly

a clue to what they might be finding objectionable. However its relatively low toxicity to adult bees versus its high toxicity to varroa mites has made it a popular treatment, this despite its toxicity to larvae, pupae and young bees, as evidenced by increased detoxifying enzyme activity and bees discarding pupal fragments. As thymol is an antiseptic, i.e. kills micro-organisms, we may wonder what its annual application is doing to the population of beneficial or symbiotic micro-organisms in the nest. It could pose a long-term threat to the integrity of the super-organism.

Beekeepers who take the plunge and sweep away medication altogether realize that they are taking risks with their colonies. Those with only one or two colonies could end up with no bees at all, so may wish to treat on a needs basis. But, for many, now that *Varroa destructor* has been present for a couple of decades, the losses are modest and tolerable. They are willing to let bee and mite co-evolve to the point of mutual adaptation in a habitation and with management that is the most bee-appropriate or bee-friendly, yet within the individual beekeeper's capability and resources, as well as conforming to local apicultural legislation. After all, bees have been around for a long time and must have long since developed behaviours for coping with ectoparasites. And indeed, we see those behaviours emerging when bees are left to tackle the mites themselves.

IS THE QUEEN STILL ROYAL?

Gunther Hauk

The honey bee queen's life raises so many questions, so much wonder and awe: miracle after miracle . . . !

The marvel starts at the beginning of the queen bee's life. Seemingly insignificant phenomena appear that determine her royalty. An egg is laid; one that could just as well become a worker bee.

The egg that is meant to become a worker is laid into a hexagonal cell and is positioned horizontally. The egg is not round; its oblong body points to the horizon for three days, before the larva hatches from the egg. Have we ever pondered what this positioning means? Every geometric shape in fact radiates an invisible field of energy that 'informs' and affects living organisms in a powerful way. What happens in nature is not accidental or haphazard but full of tremendous wisdom — even if it surpasses our modern intelligence and comprehension. At the beginning of her life, before food is given, the queen egg is already in a position and in surroundings that are radically different from the worker egg. Does this positioning have meaning, or can we simply ignore it? It seems that in the beekeeping profession no great importance is placed on this fact. Even the most modern scientific books on bees, such as the wonderfully illuminating one by Juergen Tautz,[1] only casually mention this difference.

One could say that the very fact that the worker egg is positioned horizontally for the first three days predestines the worker bee to fly out to the fields, and connect with the living surface of the earth. This horizontal plane, circling the earth from east to west, from south to north, is one we can also see as the plane allowing people to unite in the social sphere, letting us work with our fellow human beings across nations, spanning oceans and continents.

The egg that is meant to become a queen, however, is placed in a round cup, almost like the cap of an acorn, and hangs in a vertical position. This egg, for the first three to four days of her development into a queen, points in two directions, both to the centre of the earth and the centre of our solar system, to the sun. If we consider the human being, it is this vertical position that allows us to express our own sovereignty. We literally stand up for our inalienable rights; we hold our heads high. However, a psychiatrist may often have a patient lie horizontally, to access the unconscious.

We all know that conditions during the first quarter of any organism's embryonic development greatly influence its proper development and health. The fact that the bees make an early differentiation between

worker   horizontal vs. vertical   queen
         hexagonal vs. round

should tell us that there are important, albeit hidden reasons relating to the creation of a queen as opposed to worker bees.

The queen egg hatches and the future queen enters her second stage of development. Throughout this larval stage, lasting six days, she receives royal jelly, whereas the worker larvae receive it for only a few days – and even then the protein composition is different. Modern research has provided insight into the transformative power of food, and we have ample evidence that this also applies to humans. What eloquent praise we have heard in the last decades about the rejuvenating and ennobling qualities of royal jelly! Unfortunately, millions of queens are raised to the ninth day of development and then killed in order to 'harvest' royal jelly, much used in cosmetics. Not many people are aware of this practice, which should be forbidden!

The importance of a distinctive, high-quality diet in the creation of a queen is logical. But it seems that everyone erroneously points to this factor alone as causing a queen to be created from an egg which would otherwise be a worker.

After three days as an egg, and six days as a larva, the queen-to-be pupates on the ninth day, as do the workers and the drones. They all spin a cocoon of silk in which they will complete their metamorphosis into a finished insect. The drones spend 15 days in the cell as a pupa, emerging plump and strong on the 24th day. On the other hand, the workers spend only 12 days, hatching on the 21st day. This certainly makes sense, since the drones are heavier and larger than the workers.

And yet another puzzle, another miracle challenges logic. The queen, this paragon of the colony, is ready to emerge on the 16th day, after only seven days as a pupa. How do we wrap our brain around that? Rudolf Steiner's research indicates that this short span of development relates to the revolution of the sun, which, according to Steiner, takes 21 days. Through the study of sunspots it is now accepted that the sun does indeed revolve.

If we take this as a hypothesis, the drones, by exceeding this cycle, become real 'earth beings'. The workers are right there at the borderline, midway between earth and sun forces, just touching the earth, while the queen never really becomes fully integrated into earth forces. She remains, so to say, 'in the sun'. Sustained by the organism of the hive, and serving it, she never engages with the earth as such, and leaves the colony only on her marriage flight, which takes her up towards the sun, and when she swarms to create a new colony. This mating in the heights lets the strongest and at the same time lightest drones inseminate her, up to a dozen or even more. Genetic diversity and health are thus insured. Artificial insemination – for the sake of 'pure-bred' queens – falls short of nature's intention and wisdom.

After mating, the queen now has enough semen to last her for up to four or five years; and a few days after returning to the colony her reproductive organs have matured enough for her to start laying eggs.

Once again an unexpected, exceptional occurrence awaits us: the queen can lay fertilized or unfertilized eggs, both resulting in new life. When she puts her abdomen into a slightly larger cell, the queen places an unfertilized egg into it and a

drone is created. In the smaller cell, the fertilized egg will result in a worker bee. The drones are creations of virgin birth. This is also known to occur in aphids, wasps, some fishes and even a few lizards. But how the queen senses the size of the cell and chooses between fertilized and unfertilized eggs leaves us in awe and wonder.

Now comes the miracle par excellence: a queen can lay 1500 to 2000 eggs per day and, lo and behold, the weight of these eggs surpasses her own body weight! The nearly unending source of food she receives from the worker bees attending to her every need is being digested and almost instantly transformed into eggs. Is it any wonder then that the denatured food the honey bees receive from humans, in the form of sugar or corn syrup – fed to them for their winter provisions – results in a lower quality of food for the queen?

Add to this the poisons the foragers bring home with their bounty of nectar and pollen – we know that these have a cumulative effect even in the highest dilutions – and we have two major causes for the present-day epidemic of brood diseases, foul brood and chalk brood. Additional reasons are the artificial raising of queens from worker larvae, as well as the lack of a diversified diet due to medicinal 'weeds' being eliminated in our 'clean' agriculture, or more often than not, monoculture.

All of these factors are bad enough, but add to these the stress that millions of queens experience, being shipped like spark-plugs long distances and then introduced into existing colonies as strangers. Is it any wonder that within the last 45 years

queens' life expectancy has more than halved? Today, queens rarely live longer than one or two years. A side effect of this quick turnover is often ignored: the resulting youthfulness of a colony. Youth is highly valued in our modern society, but we fail to acknowledge that in our modern bee colonies a healthy maturing process is now missing, and with it the accompanying wisdom that comes with age. Resourcefulness is usually learned from life experiences, which present a diversity of problems to be solved. Youth in its exuberance tends to be more inept at coping with problems. Aren't today's bees faced with a host of challenges?

Let us now turn to a more mysterious phenomenon. Rudolf Steiner tells us in his bee lectures that the queen emits light radiation, though modern science does not acknowledge this since it is a spiritual rather than physical light. If this seems a strange idea, it might be worth remembering that light itself is a remarkable thing, and is in fact invisible until it falls upon a surface. This 'royal' radiance is perceived by the worker bees' three mysterious, tiny eyes on their foreheads. Both the pheromones the queen exudes and this light suppress the workers' ovaries from developing and maturing enough to be able to lay eggs. Worker bees are female, but their innate feminine quality to lay eggs, to create new life, is 'sacrificed' under normal conditions, when a queen is present in the colony. These workers are like nuns in an orphanage, being able to care with utter love for someone else's children, having renounced their own possible motherhood. In the same way the workers care for the queen's off-

spring, working for the well-being of the colony as a whole.

But if the queen is absent for a few days or longer, then all the workers' reproductive organs develop and some actually become 'laying' workers. If nothing is done by the beekeeper, the colony is doomed to die, since these laying workers can only lay unfertilized eggs. Soon, more and more drones will populate the hive.

The queen's royal light fills the hive, illuminating it with what we might call spiritual sunlight. I suspect that with the gradual degradation of queen bees over the last 100 years or so (artificial queen-raising was discovered toward the end of the nineteenth century and practised since then) this light and its organizing energy have been degraded as well. This results in a weakening of the queen, so that she has a harder time keeping the colony together in its function as a whole entity, an organism (see the articles by D. Heaf and M. Thiele). Add to this the attack of pesticides, herbicides and insecticides on the nerve-sense organism of the workers, resulting in disorientation, and you have at least two of the major causes of CCD. Not only have environmental degradation and poisoning contributed to the plight of honey bees, but mankind's beekeeping practices are also to blame.

It is a rude awakening to realize that our industrialized queen breeding is at the very heart of our bee crisis. From the moment the egg is laid, the physical and spiritual environment is wrong. The degradation of queens in general, over 100 generations through this practice alone, can tell us whether the queen is still really a queen. In my opinion, a clear 'NO' is the answer. Too

much of the worker element has been introduced into her. Her 'royalty' has been diminished. Food quality, stress and poisons just add to the problem. This may explain why any residual – though today sorely decimated – feral colonies tend to be healthier and more resistant than our highly manipulated domestic colonies.

It seems overwhelming and disheartening when we think of all that needs to be changed in beekeeping practices, let alone our agricultural methods, to revitalize and save our honey bees.

One difficulty in accepting change lies in the fact that we are so proud of our modern accomplishments, especially our interventionist ability to produce queens in great numbers out of worker larvae. We have convinced ourselves that this is the way to go, and we make every effort to bring our techniques to the remotest corners of the world. By doing so, we feel good about rescuing people from 'outdated' beekeeping practices.

It will take courage to make the needed changes – courage coupled with humility and a deep understanding and renewed esteem for nature's inherent wisdom. Only the acknowledgment that we have gone too far in our attempt to control and alter nature will let us take on the task of permitting swarming (very often prevented by beekeepers), so that we can have naturally raised queens again. It should be clearly stated that only in colonies preparing to swarm will natural, fully fledged queens develop, with the 'queen egg' in the right position and form from the outset.

Currently, one is considered a fool and an incompetent beekeeper when unable to stop a colony from swarming! But though 'inconvenient' for the beekeeper, it is possible to catch swarms and rehive them; and anyone who has seen a swarm will acknowledge what a marvellous sight it is: a great exhalation of bees which, like the renewal and reinvigoration we gain from our own breathing, gives both the original and the new colony a new, re-energized beginning. Working with swarms and naturally raised queens does take time and effort but will be the only way to allow the queens to regain their health and royalty.

The mechanized way of raising queens is the core issue in the harm we have caused honey bees. However, we must acknowledge that sustainable beekeeping practices altogether, not one factor alone, will return our honey bees to health and vitality. If we succeed, then the single, most important result will be: *we have a future*!

Until our agriculture turns away from destructive, life-estranged practices, it will be the task of hobby beekeepers to create islands, corridors of safety for honey bees and the other pollinators; places where the bees are cared for and nurtured, where their own needs are met and their instinctual wisdom respected. Such places will be sanctuaries in the true meaning of the word: where holistic thinking — heart thinking — creates such beauty and wholeness that the honey bee can, once again, be considered a sacred creature.

I have hope that we can turn the tide. What beekeeper is not deeply touched when seeing the queen in a hive? Our hearts jump; an outpouring of love and admiration flows to her. We wonder why this is so. Is it that we recognize in her the eternal feminine quality of creating life, of fulfilling in utter selflessness the needs of the future? We can call this her 'Sophia' being (Greek = wisdom): the hidden, deep wisdom of true royalty radiating into our lives, calling us to work *with* the laws of life.

Throughout the world a new sensitivity is awakening for the needs of other beings, a compassion for their suffering, and the will to serve the greater good. However, this new development is overshadowed by a wave of materialistic, profit-oriented thinking, still washing over us with the force of a tsunami. But no one can deny that the undertow of that wave is already tugging us in the opposite direction.

Note

1. Juergen Tautz, *The Buzz about Bees*, Springer, 2008.

Part Two
BEES AND US – THE CRISIS

Bees respond to certain powers of Nature that are extremly important and really wonderful. That is why you feel a certain reserve that will keep you from indiscriminately, and perhaps crudely, trying to put your fingers on these powers of nature. It is still true today that wherever we intrude upon these powers of nature, we tend to make things worse rather than better.

Rudolf Steiner

EARTH POEM

Jacqueline Freeman

I say to you, go back!
Our cultural memory is not so far lost
that we cannot find it again.

Stand in your field in the cool of evening
during growing season. Relax.
Swallows fly overhead,
seeds sprout, the soles of your feet
nestle in dark, rich humus,
wind wisp pollen enters your lungs,
kindles birth
in all living things.

Tell the deer you are here,
(though they already know)
tell beetle and vole beneath the soil,
that you, too, are one with this land.

You did not lose this book of earth poems,
you simply gave it away
as all farmers do,
sharing knowledge of our beloved
with all who love
without counting on return.

Spirit abounds. Knowledge roots.
The bit of Earth you stand on
remembers everything it has endured,
all that has been done to it.

Hear the farmland's prayer
that you will learn what grows best
in this land's hand.
Someday you too
will be this land's harvest.

THE FUTURE BORN FROM CRISIS

Gunther Hauk

The last 20 years have brought enormous challenges for beekeepers. The most recent one, Colony Collapse Disorder (CCD), has reached life-threatening dimensions. But we can't say we were not warned. The first indication that something had gone terribly wrong came in the 1960s, when European beekeepers experienced enormous colony losses. Since the cause for this was never found, and things seemed to return to normal, the crisis was soon forgotten.

When I got into beekeeping in the early 70s, everything was just fine. Twenty years later the parasitic varroa mite began to wreak havoc in central Europe, with many beekeepers experiencing total losses of colonies. A few years later the mite had made its way into the US. With colony losses up to 90 per cent, this was a crisis that had a bite to it. The 1996 *New York Times* article by Derrick Jensen, 'The Hush of the Hives', alarmed the public with a description of the impending danger to orchards, gardens and fields deprived of the pollination services of the honey bee.

The chemical companies were eager to fabricate solutions. We seemed to have learned nothing from Rachel Carson's book *Silent Spring*, published in the 1960s. We should have realized that these 'solutions' are, in reality, not solutions at all and would cause more problems than they solved.

At this point a critical question should have been asked: why are our honey bees not able to cope with the parasite while the Asian honey bee can? Tackling only the symptoms and failing to look at the real causes, we got another ten years' reprieve before the next crisis came. This time it was not a gentle nudge. The crisis hit with the force of a sledgehammer: Colony Collapse Disorder (CCD).

A crisis of any sort is always uncomfortable, and often painful. It creates chaos by challenging the existing order, and forces us to wake up and re-evaluate what we are doing. Change is uncomfortable and painful – especially when it is forced on us, but it opens up new perspectives that can answer the needs of the future.

Let's accept it: life is but a string of crises, starting with birth, when we give up the warm comfort of the womb. The first dentition tells us to change diet; the second prompts us to give up being a baby and get ready for school. The 'third dentition' (called moon teeth because they come out at night!) marks a stage when we can develop, if we are willing, new capacities that take us beyond the 'bite' we had developed in our professional life and become more of a giver than a taker. Then there is puberty, with all its hormonal, physical and emotional transformations. Few go through it without turmoil and chaos. If we master this one, we are prepared to handle just about every crisis to come, natural ones and self-made ones, all of which will challenge us to shed the skin of habit and comfort – and to grow.

As we live on earth, creating culture, we do inflict wounds on nature. But Mother Nature is very capable and inventive in healing her small wounds. Yet as we straighten long stretches of rivers, reduce the humus level in soils, burn vast areas of rainforest, and poison the ground water with chemicals, we create wounds that lead to unforeseen disasters. Then such catastrophes as floods, droughts, landslides and climate change provide us with a chance to wake up, to reconsider our course, and to begin healing the wounds inflicted by our damaging actions. Pain wakes us up – it raises consciousness. What a blessing! And open wounds do heal better.

A significant danger lurks in this process, however. There is often a temptation to think that the cause of a problem has nothing to do with our own actions – that the culprit is the proverbial 'other'.

Looking at crisis as a blessing in disguise let us pose the question why, over the past 100 years, we have had such an unprecedented accumulation and frequency of crises of increasing intensity. To list just a few:

- *Social crises* – not a year has gone by without wars, and some of these have involved nearly half the world
- *Deep economic crises* have shaken the very foundations of our modern banking and trading practices
- *Ecological crises* – mounting in size, ferocity and frequency

- *Health crises* – one quarter of our high-school youth experience emotional problems, one third of children in the US are overweight, and we suffer life-threatening diseases of epidemic proportions
- *Cultural crises* – such as women's rights, child slave labour, drug abuse, unemployment, and an increasing absence of ethical and moral conscience among some business and political leaders.

Considering that approximately 60 per cent of all animal and plant species on this globe have been brought to extinction in the last 150 years, how many of us are aware of the full dimensions of our ecological crisis? Before we continue on this crazy path of destruction, it seems that we need a big crisis to wake us up – one that will touch many people's hearts, and take the alarm level from orange to red. Well, now we have just that: the honey bees are disappearing. We have Colony Collapse Disorder!

If we think that by identifying bacteria, viruses, fungi, mites or beetles as the cause of this crisis, and by eliminating them we can solve the problem, then we are barking up the wrong tree. These are merely symptoms of a weakened organism lacking the vitality to fight off these intruders. The causes must be found at a deeper level.

Generally speaking, we can acknowledge that our great technological, industrial and mechanical accomplishments, as useful as they are, have a dark side, which we tend to ignore. Yes, it is true that the mechanization of our lives saves us time and has brought us comfort and ease (though paradoxically, many of us are busier than ever). Nobody wants to stop turning on the lights with a flick of a switch or walk the distances we now drive or fly. Still, the comfort we have achieved has not solved our social problems…

Where we have gone wrong is to uncritically apply the laws of mechanics and technology to realms where different laws rule, namely to the realm of life. Applying them to their own realm is appropriate. The entire realm of agriculture has especially suffered from this wrongful application. Farming has become a factory enterprise where specialization and mechanization rule. The laws governing life, however, demand diversification, complexity and respect for the inherent needs of each organism. Likewise they demand respect and understanding for the synergies at work in the finely tuned, delicate interplay of almost unlimited patterns, rhythms and influences. During the last 150 years, our reductionist, simplistic understanding of nature has thoroughly supplanted a previous holistic one. Devastating effects can be witnessed wherever life is manipulated according to the now ruling paradigm.

It is this materialistic, one-track thinking that has also brought the honey bees – and with them the other pollinators – to the edge of an abyss. What have we done to the bees? For reasons of commercial gain as well as convenience, we have sapped their life forces and undermined their immune system. Thus, we have made them vulnerable to viruses, bacteria and fungi – organisms whose specific task is to eliminate those who are weak.

Let's look at some present-day beekeeping practices and consider:

- the standardized Langstroth hive body with removable frames
- the wired wax foundations; some now even made of plastic
- the artificial feeding of sugar and corn syrup
- the artificial breeding of queens from worker larvae
- the suppression of swarming
- the trucking of over half of professionally managed colonies from one monoculture to the next, with some hives now travelling over 100,000 miles each year

These factors alone would be sufficient to overtax these hypersensitive creatures – without considering also the huge impact chemicals and pesticides have on bees.

All of these methods have been invented and perfected to maximize our honey production and the pollination of huge monoculture acreages. Not one of these modern beekeeping methods has had the honey bees' health and vitality in mind! An advertisement for plastic foundations in recent years sums up an underlying motive for many of these inventions: '*We asked some bees what would make them more profitable*'.

Mankind absolutely needs the honey bees, since they, together with ants, hornets, wasps and other species of bees, are *the* source of sustainability and biodiversity. Not only is the honey bee such an excellent pollinator due to its overwintering as a colony – ready at the end of winter to fly out in great numbers – but the formic acid poison that honey bees produce, and constantly spread in very dilute form as they collect nectar and pollen, wonderfully invigorates all plant life.[1]

We may not have learned it in school, but it is a fact that acids are the very foundation of all life processes: think DNA, amino acids, fatty acids, and peptic acid, just to name a few. Formic acid, in its homeopathic dilution, is as essential to life as oxygen, carbon, hydrogen and all the other chemicals about which we seem to know much more.

And the stinging insects are the source of this life elixir. There is no doubt that we have to expand our horizon and re-evaluate our relationship with these insects. We need to regain our awe and wonder, and gratitude for their service. Ignorance currently still prevails, resulting in fear of and aggression against these *givers of life*.

It has frequently been said that the honey bee is the 'canary in the coalmine'. Canaries, of course, were used to warn of the build-up of gases in mines and thus of the impending danger of an explosion. When the bird stopped singing (and usually dropped dead), it was time to get out quick. Now, as honey bees die in huge numbers without a single clear cause, I believe they can wake us up to the danger threatening our very existence. We must change the way we look at and work with nature. Their alarming, poignant plight is asking us to face what we have been doing by focusing entirely on commercial interests and the mechaniza-tion of all aspects of beekeeping. Unfortu-nately we are doing the same throughout agriculture – for example to our cows, pigs and chickens. These animals are all experiencing tremendous suffering due to factory farming methods.

The exploitative mindset is not exclusive to professional beekeepers. Systematically, such methods have found their way into hobby beekeeping circles. At beekeepers meetings one still hears questions such as, 'How many pounds did you get from your hives this year?' We cannot pose such a question and, at the same time, claim to have a loving, nurturing relationship with these creatures.

But there are positives. The rapid growth in backyard and rooftop beekeepers and the growing number of individuals want-ing to help honey bees is a sure sign that the CCD crisis has been an enormous help in raising new consciousness and con-science, and in starting a shift towards a more holistic understanding of nature.

But the critical questions, in my opinion, are not yet answered: will we be able to go deep enough in our understanding to help us really reverse our habits in time, giving up some of our comforts and changing our addiction to herbicides and pesticides? Or will we continue in more or less the same way, in the same mindset, failing to accept the crisis as an opportunity for learning and for potentially radical change.

Some may hope to solve the problem with an illusory silver bullet, by trying to breed a *super-bee* that can withstand all our exploitation, our poisons, and our depleted nectar and pollen supply. In this scenario, the ensuing crisis is likely to hit with the force of weapons of mass destruction, not least because we fail to address real underlying problems in our whole relationship with the natural world.

The alternative is to use the crisis to become true stewards and caretakers of nature's beings; then we will be able – with

nature's help – to cultivate the harmony of true interdependence, and continue on our evolutionary path.

We need a paradigm shift that is as enormous as the one 600 years ago at the dawn of modernity. At that time, we gradually began to lose our spiritual understanding of nature, of the human being, and limited ourselves increasingly to materialistic and analytic explorations and understanding. The difference between these two turning points in evolution is that the present one threatens our very existence.

It is interesting that one of the most remarkable scientists of the twentieth century, Albert Einstein, indicated the change that is necessary for solving all of our ongoing crises:

> Imagination is more important than knowledge. For knowledge is limited, whereas imagination embraces the entire world, stimulating progress, giving birth to evolution. It is, strictly speaking, a real factor in scientific research... We cannot solve problems with the same mindset that created them.[2]

Only through training our power of imagination, and through a renewed sense of awe, reverence and wonder for all that exists, will we be able to heal the deep separation and estrangement from nature we are experiencing in our times. I am deeply convinced that no 'solutions' offered by the multinational chemical companies will work!

It is high time to admit, based on what we have witnessed, that not everything which our creative minds invent is safe and good. We must seek guidance and wisdom that only our heart possesses while preserving our logical faculties of discernment, developed especially over the last 600 years. We must learn anew that it is love, not control, which has the ultimate power to further life on earth.

Let us not despair in this crisis. I personally choose to view the present shake-up as the greatest possible stimulus and opportunity for a new order. When we wake up to the pain we are inflicting, our heart begins to govern and inspire the deeds that alone will ensure a safe future.

Notes

1. See Rudolf Steiner, *Bees*, Anthroposophic Press, 1998, pp. 133–7.
2. A. Einstein, *Cosmic Religion: With Other Opinions and Aphorisms*, 1931, p. 97.

HOW ARE GENETICALLY ENGINEERED CROPS AFFECTING HONEY BEES?

Interview with Jeffrey Smith

Bees all over the world are suffering colony decline. We believe that there are many aspects of industrial agriculture impacting on the health of honey bees, with pesticides at the forefront. But the worst of the colony collapse disorders are happening in the United States. Why is it worse there than Germany, France or elsewhere? The United States has so many millions of acres of genetically engineered crops, which we believe might be a contributing factor, causing the loss of bees here to be greater than in other parts of the world.

There are very few studies on this, but one piece of research compared bees that were collecting pollen from corn (maize) genetically engineered to produce its own insecticide, compared to bees collecting pollen from natural non-GMO corn fields. Those that visited the GM corn got sick; they got an infectious disease, while the control group did not. This suggests that genetically engineered crops can compromise the immune system of bees.

In addition, one German scientist found that when bees pollinate genetically engineered corn the gene inserted into the corn ends up transferring into the gut microorganisms of the bees and continues to function. What this means is that we could have long-term impact from short-term exposure. Unfortunately, human beings also get genes transferred to their gut bacteria. The only human feeding study showed that genes inserted into soybeans transfer into the DNA of our intestinal flora and appear to continue functioning there. In other words, genetically engineered bacteria continue to reproduce GM proteins inside us.

In addition, bees are often fed over the wintertime with high fructose corn syrup, which itself is created from genetically engineered corn. So they're getting hit with the effects from the GMOs from every corner.

Their immune system — our warning system

Everyone knows the importance of bees. When there's a massive die-off of bees politicians, the community, everyone really wakes up and realizes this is a not just a national but a global emergency. It is a food emergency, a nature emergency. Bees are very delicate. Their immune system is not particularly strong and so they are early indicators of the health of our ecosystem.

Now, it is fortunate in this sense, oddly enough, that bees have a delicate immune system and that they can warn us that something is wrong. If there were colony collapse among other types of insects that we didn't rely on for pollination or food production, that would not, in our arrogance, register with us. But we can't afford to let the bees go. So they are in a sense sacrificing themselves as a wake-up call. They're dying in huge numbers and we now have to pay attention because our food supply is at risk. They're calling our attention to huge imbalances in our ecosystem.

I have been disappointed, so far, with the amount of money that has been allocated by the US government to finding the source of the problem. Here you find corporate control of government purse strings. We've been tracing it, and it turns out pesticide producers, and the GMO producers, don't want the government to do deep investigation into bee health because it will end up implicating their products and force them off the market. But we don't have the luxury of waiting for more bees to die and leaving our whole pollination system in peril.

These days, bees are migrant farm workers. They're one of the unsung heroes of agriculture. Every year, huge hive trucks descend on California's almond tree region and the bees are used to pollinate the trees. But if the bees' immune system is compromised and they develop more susceptibility to certain infections, then one colony coming into the California region could theoretically infect many other bee hives; and so you end up in a situation where the nation is running a beekeeping system that will really test and challenge the immune system of all the bees. It *is* challenged — and it is failing.

GMOs and pesticides

There's a lot of information about the risks of GMOs. Corn and cotton plants in the United States are engineered to produce what's called Bt toxin — from soil bacteria called *Bacillus thuringiensis*. The toxin produced by the bacteria is toxic and kills certain insects. Some farmers use the natural bacterial form as a pesticidal spray; but in this case the Bt gene is not forced into the DNA of corn and cotton plants, so that every cell produces an even more toxic version of the Bt poison, at concentrations equal to thousands of times the spray form. Theoretically this could cause significant harm to bee health around the United States, as well as globally.

Alongside the risk from GMOs there is also pesticide treatment of seeds. Pesticide is put in the seeds themselves; it is time-released, to remain throughout the young plant for an extended period. These nicotine-based seed treatments, known as the class of neonicotinoids, can certainly cause problems with bee health. When exposed, bees can lose their ability to find their way back to their hives.

This correlates with Colony Collapse Disorder. Beekeepers basically discover that some of their hives are empty. The bees are mysteriously gone. The loss can be catastrophic. It can be 50 or even 90 per cent of the hives. I read recently that about one third of all bees in the United States have been killed recently due to this mysterious disorder.

Scientists wondered how the bees were exposed to these systemic pesticides in plants. They have discovered that there is a liquid secreted in droplets by the plants in the morning. Bees drink from these drop-lets, and are thus exposed to the neo-nicotinoids.

France is finally getting rid of these pesticide-treated seeds. Germany, in May 2008, also declared such seed treatment illegal. They know it can kill bees. But the authorities in the USA refuse to act. In fact, certain GMO corn seeds have as much as five times the levels of these neonico-tinoids. So they have both a built-in gene that produces the Bt toxin *and* are treated with high levels of these pesticides – in one stroke doubling the potential impact on bees.

Dangerous GMOs found in honey

I've worked with more than 30 scientists over two years to document all the known health risks from GMOs. We found 65 risks. GMOs are linked to thousands of toxic and allergic reactions in humans, thousands of sick, sterile and dead live-stock and damage to virtually every organ and every system studied in lab animals. So of course the bees are at risk. They have direct contact with genetically engineered pollen. They have direct contact with the nectar and water produced by these crops. And the impact on bees is not adequately considered when these crops are being developed and put into the environment.

As you may know, beekeepers in Europe were told by the authorities that 'GMOs are no problem in corn' because bees don't collect nectar from it. But bees *do* collect *pollen* from corn. And every honey in Europe must have pollen in it in order to be

called honey. A study found that one third of all the honey produced by bees raised near genetically engineered corn contained genetically engineered components due to contamination from pollen collected by foraging bees.

Honey and bee products have incredible healing properties. Api-therapy is a regi-men in which bees are placed on the acu-puncture points of patients and induced to sting those areas. I am told this has even been found to help in cases of MS. Honey too has long been known to have medicinal properties.

But if you change the structure and constituents of honey, royal jelly and pro-polis through genetically engineered pollen and genetically engineered nectar, you're adding a potentially disastrous element that could cancel out the positive elements of bee products. And no one is looking at this.

The bee as second-class citizen

There are co-existence rules in Europe whereby people try to figure out a plan to allow GMOs to exist alongside non-GMOs, given cross-pollination and seed mixing. Recent German legislation completely ignored bees in their co-existence plan, and so parliament told the legislative or executive branch that they have to go back and include bees in their co-existence policies. But here's the problem: how are you going to tell the bees not to pollinate genetically modified crops?

You see, in a sense, bees are considered second-class citizens. They're not protected by law. They shouldn't be a second thought but a first thought. They're absolutely essential as pollinators. They bestow on us the fantastic products of their non-stop work. And they're also our early warning system of ecological degradation. The impact on bee population and bee health shows that we need to act now — and by doing so will find we are protecting our own health as well.

The natural world just 'background noise'?

There was a discovery years ago that the monarch butterfly may be at risk due to the planting of genetically modified corn. And the response of the US department of agriculture spokesperson to this was, 'Well, we just consider these problems as background noise.' But we can't think about bee deaths as background noise. We need to rally around bee health, around bee vitality. Because when we create an ecosystem that supports the delicate immune system of these creatures it will also better support ourselves.

I think that bees have a lot of lessons to teach us. And, as someone focused on genetically modified foods, they've taught us that genes transfer to bacteria: they do in bees, they do in humans. They have shown us that pesticides can be deadly to both bees and humans. And I think now

they are showing us that genetically modified crops can also be devastating to bees and humans.

Taking back agriculture from the big corporations

We need to study natural, harmless agriculture. We need to put money into that, rather than into the corporate-driven model of agriculture. What's happening to the bees is really a symptom of the corporate control of governments in the world right now. They are pushing their particular agenda irrespective of what happens in terms of the side effects on humans, animals, insects or flora.

We need to remove control from the corporations whose only concern is their own profits, and place responsibility for custodianship of the natural world in the hands of those who can put the interests of nature and the bees before profit. This is also ultimately in our own interest. We must love bees, we must take care of them for their sakes, but also for ours. And if they're dying something is seriously wrong.

However superior we think ourselves, the bees are currently telling us that we cannot go on transgressing against nature for much longer. It is high time for change.

PESTICIDES, GMOS AND THE WAR AGAINST BIODIVERSITY

Dr. Vandana Shiva

In 1992, when farmers of Karnataka destroyed Cargill's seed processing plant because Cargill's sunflower seeds had failed, the chief of Cargill for the Asia Pacific area responded by saying the farmers were stupid because they were rejecting technology that 'prevented bees from usurping the pollen'.

When bees and pollinators on whom we depend for our very survival are perceived as thieves, the war against biodiversity is being waged in earnest.

The toxic legacy of the 'Green Revolution': from Punjab to Bhopal

The year 1984 woke me up to the fact that something was terribly wrong with the way food was being produced. With the violence in Punjab and operation Blue Star, and the disaster in Bhopal, agriculture looked like war, even though the Green Revolution in India – based on toxic chemicals – had been awarded a Nobel Peace Prize. That is when I started to study the Green Revolution and wrote *The Violence of the Green Revolution*. And this is why I started Navdanya as a movement for an agriculture free of poisons and toxins.

The Green Revolution has been sold to us as a miracle which increased food production. However, it did not produce more food overall, because food includes cereals and pulses and oil seeds and vegetables, not just rice and wheat. Crop diversity was destroyed to create the chemical monocultures of rice and wheat. Overall, nutrition per acre went down, and toxins per acre went up. The Green Revolution myth is based on hiding both the food production lost and the costs of the burden of environmental toxicity that Punjab must bear to provide toxic food to the nation.

Today, Punjab is the toxic capital of India. The monocultures of rice and wheat are a perfect breeding ground for pests. And the use of toxic pesticides has continued to escalate in Punjab. While pests are not a problem in ecologically balanced agriculture, in an unstable agricultural system they pose a series of challenges to agronomy. The metaphor for pesticide use in agriculture then becomes 'war', as an introduction to a textbook on pest management illustrates:

> The war against pests is a continuing one that man must fight to ensure his survival. The war story describes some of the battles that have been fought; and the continuing guerrilla war [describes] the type of enemies we are facing, and some of the manoeuvres for survival.[1]

However, seeing biodiversity as an 'enemy' in a war waged with lethal chemical weapons is wrong for two reasons. Firstly, it fails to control pests. Secondly, the toxics boomerang to harm humans, since humans are part of the food chain.

Poison for profits

Pesticides, which in fact started as war chemicals, have failed to control pests. They have instead led to the emergence of new pests, and the development of resistance in old pests, requiring increased pesticide use. Pesticides create pests by destroying the pest-predator balance.

Having failed to control pests through the Green Revolution, the pesticide industry then introduced the second Green Revolution based on genetically engineered seeds; Punjab is one of the regions where Bt cotton has been introduced.[2] Bt crops are implanted with a gene for producing a toxin introduced with them. The plant itself becomes a pesticide factory, continually producing toxins in every cell. Yet genetic engineering has also failed as a technology for controlling pests. The bollworm, which it was supposed to control, has evolved resistance and now pests are emerging every year. The result is a 13-fold increase in pesticide use. The farmers suffer twice over. Costly seeds and costly chemicals push them into a debt trap, and debt pushes them to suicide. *Over 200,000 farmers have committed suicide in India since 1997.*

Farmers' suicides

On 8 September 2006, nine farmers' union teams in Punjab organized a public hear-ing on farmers' suicides. I was invited as a member of the citizens' jury. The Diwan Hall of Gurdwara Haaji Rattan was over-flowing with a sea of people – all family members of suicide victims. The farmers' organizations had collected information on 2860 suicides, and mobilized family members to give evidence at the public hearing. This was building on an earlier public hearing organized by Navdanya on 1 and 2 April 2006.

The suicides are most frequent where farmers grow cotton and have been a direct result of the creation of seed monopolies.

Increasingly, the supply of cotton seeds has slipped out of the hands of the farmers and the public system, into the hands of global seed corporations like Monsanto. Corporate seed supply implies a number of shifts simultaneously:

- Giant corporations start to control local seed companies through buyouts, joint ventures and licensing arrangements, leading to a seed monopoly.
- Seed is transformed from being a common good to being the 'intellectual property' of a corporation, for which it can claim limitless profits through royalty payments. For the farmer this means deeper debt.
- Seed is transformed from a renewable regenerative, multiplicative resource into a non-renewable resource and commodity. Seed scarcity and seed farmers are a consequence of seed monopolies, which are based on renewability of seed, beginning with hybrids, moving to genetically engineered seed like Bt-cotton, with the ultimate aim of the 'terminator' seed

which is engineered for sterility. Each of these technologies of non-renewability is guided by one factor alone – forcing farmers to buy seed every planning season. For farmers this means higher costs. For seed corporations it translates into higher profits.

- The creation of seed monopolies is based on simultaneous deregulation for seed corporations, including bio-safety and seed deregulation, and super-regulation of farmers' seeds and varieties. Globalization allowed seed companies to sell self-certified seeds. In the case of genetically engineered seed, they are seeking self-regulation for bio-safety. This is the main aim of the recently proposed National Biotechnology Regulatory Authority, which is in effect a Bio-safety 'Deregulation Authority'! The proposed Seed Bill 2004, blocked by a massive, nationwide Gandhian Seed Satyagraha (= 'Fight for Truth') by farmers, aims at forcing every farmer to register the varieties they have evolved over millennia. This compulsory registration and licensing system robs farmers of their fundamental freedoms.
- Corporate seeds impose monocultures on farmers. Mixed croppings of cotton with cereals, legumes, oil-seeds, vegetables is replaced with a monoculture of Bt-cotton hybrids.

The creation of seed monopolies and with it the creation of unpayable debt to a new species of money lender, the agents of the seed and chemical companies, has led to hundreds of thousands of Indian farmers killing themselves since 1997.

Peasants in Warangal used to grow millets, pulses, oil-seeds. Overnight, Warangal was converted to a cotton-growing district based on non-renewable hybrids which need irrigation and are prone to pest attacks. Small peasants without capital were trapped in a vicious cycle of debt.

A few case histories

To show how farmers are paying for corporate-led globalization with their lives, the Navdanya organization brought out its report *Seeds of Suicide*. Below are a few instances of appalling misery caused by unsustainable, corporate-led agriculture.

Sukhbir Singh, aged 42, of Chak Sadoke, Ferozepur District, ended his life on 26 October 2003 by jumping into a river because he was unable to pay a debt of 1.9 million rupees despite selling seven acres of land. He left behind a widow and two children.

Harjinder Singh, aged 21, of Ratla Thark, who lost his seven acres to money-lenders, ended his life by consuming pesticides. And 60-year-old Jeet Singh of the same village burnt himself to death.

Hardev Singh, aged 28, of Urmmat Puria in Hoga drank pesticide on 12 July 2002 when he could not clear his loan of 0.7 million rupees even after selling eight acres; 26-year-old Avatar Singh of Machika Village died on 28 March 2006 after consuming pesticide; 48-year-old Jagtar Singh of Doda in Mukstar left behind a widow and daughter after drinking pesticide to end his life – he had sold two acres to partially pay a debt of 150,000 rupees.

Raghubir Singh, aged 28, mortgaged

four acres, could not clear his loan, and ended his life on 28 April 2004 by consuming pesticide. His mother, widow and two children were left to struggle on their own.

The names were different, the faces were different, but the tragedy was the same: the avoidable tragedy of poisoning farmers' fields and lives for profit, and the legacy of this for farmers' wives and children.

Suicide by drinking the lethal and debt-creating pesticide took the lives of

Gurjit's husband Budh Singh
Baljit Kaur's husband Thail Singh
Karamjit's husband Bhola Singh
Manjit Kaur's husband Sunder Singh
Gurmeet's husband Gudu Singh
Paramjit's husband Pritpal
Gurdayal Kaur's husband Jarnail Singh
Sukhpal's husband Gurcharan Singh
Jeet Kaur's husband Gurmeet Singh
Malkeet's husband Nishatar,
Tel Kaur's husband Nirpal
Sarabjit's husband Prem Singh
Jagat Kaur's husband Balbir
Surjeet Kaur's husband Dilwar Singh
Kulwinder Kaur's husband Sindoore Singh
Manjir Kaur's husband Chattar Singh
Amarjeet's husband Pappi
Jasbir's husband Nirpesh Singh
Sukhdev Kaur's husband Birpal
Paramjeet's husband Pappi Singh
Sukhdev Kaur's husband Balwant Singh
Daljit Kaur's husband Sumukh
Harbans Kaur's son Gurmeet
Baldev Kaur's son Mewa Singh
Beant Kaur's husband Jailer Singh
Tej Kaur's husband Buttu Singh
Jasbir Kaur's son Jagga Singh
Tej Kaur's husband Mitti Singh
Jasbir Kaur's husband Kishan Singh
Charanjeet Kaur's husband Mahadev Singh

and thousands more...

As I heard unending stories from widows of how they had lost their dear ones, their land, their hopes in the vicious cycle of debt, my mind went back to 1984. I started to ask questions about the Green Revolution and the violence of extremism and terrorism that had overtaken this prosperous and proud 'land of five rivers' (the meaning of 'Punjab').

If not suicide, cancer...

Those who do not fall prey to suicide in Punjab are dying of cancer. There is a 'cancer' train that leaves Punjab to treat villagers in Punjab suffering from cancer in a charitable hospital in Bikaner. This toxic economy is another 'gift' of the Green Revolution, as was the tragedy of Bhopal. The gas leak in Bhopal that killed thousands in December 1984 was from the pesticide plant of Union Carbide. Pesticides are designed to kill – and from Punjab to Bhopal they have killed thousands of human beings.

Our bread basket in Punjab does not have to be an epicentre of toxicity. The people of Bhopal did not need to die. There is a non-violent alternative to the violence of the first and second Green Revolutions. It is bio-diverse organic farming which we practise and promote through Navdanya. Contrary to the propaganda, bio-diverse ecological systems produce food and nutrition far better and far more sustainably than chemical monocultures.

It is time to give up the false model of food security which is killing our children through malnutrition, killing our farmers through debt, and killing people from Punjab to Bhopal because of the unnecessary use of toxic poisons in farming. We can be free of both hunger and toxics.

Bt crops: putting the pesticide into the plant

Bt toxins are a family of related molecules produced in nature by a soil bacterium, *Bacillus thuringiensis*. Farmers and gardeners have used natural Bt as an organic pesticide for more than 50 years. But Bt genes are now being genetically engineered into crops so that the plant produces toxins throughout most of its life.

Genetically engineered Bt crops are being offered as a sustainable pest-control strategy. However, they are neither ecological nor sustainable. They are not ecological because internalizing toxin production in plants is not a toxin-free strategy – it merely produces toxins within plants rather than applying them externally. The ecological impact of this strategy of internalizing toxins has not been fully researched, though indications are emerging that genetically engineered Bt is harmful to beneficial insects such as bees and ladybirds.

The Bt crop strategy is not a sustainable method for pest control because Bt plants release toxins continuously. Constant long-term exposure of pest populations to Bt encourages survival of individual pests that are genetically resistant to the toxin. As Margaret Mellon and Jane Rissler of the Union of Concerned Scientists state in their report *Now or Never*.[3]

> Over many generations, the proportion of resistant individuals in pest populations can increase, reducing the efficacy of the Bt toxin as pesticide. If resistance evolves, Bt toxins will cease to be effective both for the users of the new transgenic plants and those who have relied on Bt sprays for decades. Scientists have estimated that widespread use of Bt crops could lead to the loss of Bt's efficacy against certain pest populations in as few as two to five years.

The primary justification for the genetic engineering of Bt into crops is that this will reduce the use of insecticides. One corporate sales brochure had a picture of a few worms and stated, 'You will see these in your cotton and that's O.K. Don't spray.' However, in Texas a lawsuit was filed by 25 farmers over Bt cotton planted on 18,000 acres, which suffered cotton bollworm damage and on which farmers had to use pesticides in spite of corporate propaganda that genetic engineering meant an end to the pesticide era. In 1996, 2 million acres in the USA were planted with Bt transgenic cotton. Yet cotton bollworms were found to have infested thousands of acres planted with the new breed of cotton. Not only did the genetically engineered cotton not survive cotton bollworm attack, the strategy will create super-bugs by inducing Bt-resistance in pests. The question is not *whether* super-pests will be created, but when they will become dominant.

The US Environment Protection Agency (EPA) requires four per cent 'refugia' of non-engineered crops to be planted near the engineered crops. This acts as a refuge for insects to survive and breed, with the aim of lowering overall resistance in the insect population – reflecting the reality of the creation of resistant strains of insects. Yet even with a four per cent refugia level, insect resistance will evolve in as little as three to four years. For Bt corn, likewise, a three per cent 'sacrificial' refugia is proposed. Thus, farmers have to make a major sacrifice to adopt the new 'miracle' crops of genetic engineering. The build-up of pest-resistance also undermines the use of *natural* Bt in organic agriculture.

This is why legal action was filed against the US EPA in Washington by Greenpeace International, the International Federation of Organic Movements (world organization of organic farmers, producers and retailers in over 100 countries), the Sierra Club, the National Family Farm Coalition, California Certified Organic Farmers, the Rural Advancement Foundation International (RAFI), the Institute for Agriculture and Trade Policy and over 20 organic farmers' organizations. The central demands of the suit were that the EPA should cancel registration of all genetically engineered plants containing the Bt pesticide, and refrain from taking new registrations. Furthermore, it demanded that the EPA complete an impact statement analysing registration of genetically engineered plants that express Bt.

Engineering a toxin into a plant clearly has its own hazards. Plants engineered to manufacture their own pesticides can harm organisms other than their intended targets. Soil-inhabiting organisms that degrade organic matter containing the insecticidal toxins produced by the Bt bacterium can be harmed by the toxin.

The giant corporations have agreements to share patented genetically engineered seed traits with each other. These seed corporations are not competing with each other. They are competing with peasants and farmers over the control of the seed supply.

And back to the bees and insects...

Corporate promotional literature does not inform farmers about the risks of Bt crops. Hendrik Verfaillie, the then President of Monsanto, stated in an address to the Forum on Nature and Human Society at the National Academy of Sciences, Washington DC on 30 October 1997 (describing Monsanto's Bt potato):

> The bio engineered plant has been given genetic instructions which allow it to use sunshine, air and soil nutrients to make a biodegradable protein that affects specific insects and pests, and only those individual insects that actually take a bite of the plant... It spares the lives of the beneficial insects which previously would have been killed by broadcasting a broad spectrum insecticide.

This description is misleading in many ways. To say that the impact is artificially restricted to insects 'that take a bite of the plant' overlooks the impact on bees that take the pollen, and *organisms that eat the insects which have eaten the toxin*. The impact of Bt crops can be large because the toxin can travel up the food chain and is hence not limited to the plant and insects that feed on it.

Chemical insecticides were pushed in the developing world on the grounds that without them agricultural production is impossible. However, as the experience of Indonesia shows, a reduction of pesticides by 60 per cent contributed to an *increase* of rice yields by 13 per cent.[4]

Genetic engineering is creating new forms of genetic pollution. Across the world evidence is emerging about the reality of the threat from this new form of pollution. The nature of genetic pollution is of a different order from that of chemical pollution in the enduring and multiplying nature of the damage it causes.

According to evidence presented by the Union of Concerned Scientists, there are already signals that the commercial-scale use of some transgenic crops poses serious ecological risks and does not deliver the industry's promises. The insecticidal Bt-toxins are often engineered into plants in a pre-activated form, and are already known to be harmful to bees directly, and to lacewings further up the food chain. A study in Switzerland found that lacewings, which prey on corn pests, suffered mal-development and increased mortality when fed with corn borers raised on a Bt crop (Hilbech et al., 1998).

Nothing is yet known of the impact on human health when toxin-producing Bt crops such as potato and corn are eaten, or on animal health when oilcake from Bt-cotton or fodder from Bt corn is consumed as cattle feed. But research by Scottish Crop Research showed that ladybirds fed on aphids which were fed on transgenic potatoes laid fewer eggs and lived half as long as ladybirds on a normal diet (Brich et al., 1996/97). Another piece of research that sent shock waves throughout the scientific and environmental community is the finding by Cornell scientists that the monarch butterfly *Danaus plexippus* was killed by ingesting milkweed leaves dusted with pollen from Bt cotton (Losey et al., 1999).

Technologies are tools. When the tool fails it needs replacing. Bt-cotton technology has failed to control pests or secure farmers' lives and livelihoods. It is time to replace GM technology with ecological farming. It is time to stop farmers' suicides.

It is time to stop seeing bees and pollinators as our enemies. They are our friends. They are our family. Farming is not a war against nature but harmonious collaboration and co-existence with it. Farming should not be big business that drives farmers to suicide or gives them cancer, but the vital foundation for human life. Agriculture can nurture nature and promote biodiversity. At present it is destroying nature and human beings – all of us – who depend on it.

Notes

1. W. Fletcher, *The Pest War*, Basil Blackwell, Oxford 1974, p. 1.
2. *Bacillus thuringiensis* – see p. 96 and also interview with Jeffrey Smith.
3. Fred and Bruce, 1998.
4. In: L.A. Trupp, *New Partnerships for Sustainable Agriculture*, World Resources Institute, 1997.

THE WEB OF BEING

Interview with Vandana Shiva

I've always embedded my own thinking and action in the concept of an earth democracy. And we have a wonderful word for it in Sanskrit: *Vasudhaiva kutumbkham* (= 'earth family'). *Vasudhaiva* is the earth goddess, and *kutumbkham* is her family. And her family includes the earthworms and soil microbes, the flying ones and the four-legged ones and the two-legged ones; and the bees are very much part of that earth family. An earth democracy embedded in that thinking means you don't begin by believing it is your right to exploit others. It means you're fully aware that they're your extended family; and just as you would not go around butchering your children or murdering your mother, you should make sure that every life form has its space, is protected.

In the last few decades and centuries our thinking has been shaped by *my* rights, by greed and capitalism in which the world is an object to be exploited, and nothing lives but is all dead matter. Everything is an instrument, and productiveness means destroying biodiversity, in the false belief you will gain from this. Authentic democracy, by contrast, is based on responsibility for the other, for every last being; and I do feel the bee is one of these last beings. Well, you know the relation between the seeds and bees and pollinators is for me very fascinating. We've brought back seed diversity on our farm and we grow more

than 1,000 varieties including 500 rice varieties. But the 42 seed banks across the country have also rescued about 3,000 varieties.

Now, every farm that has biodiversity and has a wide range of varieties is farming ecologically. These are sanctuaries for the pollinators. I think we've increased pollinator population at least tenfold in the last 15 years since we started to save diversity – because different pollinator species need different plants.

Industrial farming is based on chemicals derived originally from warfare, designed to kill human beings. But of course they kill pollinators. The tremendous death of bees that we are seeing is I believe partly due to the very intensive use of pesticides. For example, the crazy way of controlling one kind of moth that is being proposed in California would kill hundreds of other kinds of pollinators. And genetically engineered crops with Bt[1] toxin in them is, I think, an issue that hasn't been assessed enough even though very early in the day at Cornell a study was done that showed Bt pollen kills butterflies. After all, pollinators live on pollen. They transmit pollen. That's how they hybridize. That's how they maintain the future fertility of seed.

This generation of seed is transformed into the next generation of seed only through the gift of the pollinator. Seeds that you can save and harvest and plant again are called 'open pollinated' varieties because bees and butterflies pollinate them. They are open to pollination. Get rid of the bees and butterflies and you have to use the equivalent of artificial crop insemination. Then the last stage is genetic engineering, where you take genes from an unrelated species and shoot it into the cells of a plant. There are only two ways you can introduce unrelated genes. The first is by using a gene gun, to shoot gene-laden gold particles into the organism. But this is a very unreliable process so you also have to add antibiotic resistance markers and viral promoters; and every genetically engineered seed is a bundle of bacteria, toxins and viral promoters. The other way of introducing genes, unrelated genes, is through cancer infections. And the scientists are telling us that this itself can be a source of new disease.

The entire technology of breeding in the last century in the United States, and the rest of the world in the last few decades, is I believe a technology for breeding scarcity. The beauty of the seed is that out of one you can get millions. The beauty of the pollinator is that it does the work of turning that one into a million. And that's an economics of abundance, of renewability, an economics of mutuality. That to me is the real economics of growth, because life means growth and abundance. By contrast, the economics and technology of artificial hybridization, of genetic modification, is a deliberate creation of scarcity. You prevent the pollinators from pollinating, you prevent one seed from growing into a million. And you do that so that farmers are forced to come and buy seed every year. The growth here is of profits for companies like

Monsanto but in fact it leads to scarcity, ever greater impoverishment of life's abundance.

I think there are a number of reasons the bees are threatened hugely. Personally as a scientist I see three very plausible explanations for Colony Collapse Disorder, none of which are mutually exclusive, and all of which could be playing a role. One is the heavy use of pesticides and another the spread of Bt crops. Bt after all is a toxin. And now the toxin is engineered into the plant and is releasing this toxin in its cells all the time in a way very different from the natural form of the bacteria, where it becomes a toxin only in the gut of particular insects in interaction with particular enzymes. So now we have ready-made toxins over millions of acres in India. If the goats are dying from eating it, then surely bees will be dying too. A farmer growing this Bt cotton illegally in the state of Horisabay, where it hasn't been approved, was arrested for causing the death of goats. Now if farmers are being arrested because goats are dying I think Monsanto should be arrested for the killing of bees and pollinators. They're putting the future of Creation at stake. Not just the future of bees, but the future of humanity and future of all life.

The third possible cause is radiation. I may be more sensitive to this because I live in a rural environment. I feel there's pollution from all these new electromagnetic waves that are making our communication systems smart. We are not looking at the impact electromagnetic radiation may be having on life and specifically how it may be interfering with bees, which are highly and subtly attuned to their environment.

We have learnt how to recognize the pollution of 200 years ago, the carbon dioxide from fossil fuels. It took us 200 years of stupidity and blindness to wake up to the impact of fossil fuel industrialism on the planet's climate. I do not think we should wait another 200 years. We do not *have* another 200 years to find out what genetic pollution and electromagnetic pollution could be doing to life on earth. You know, I've been trained as a physicist, and I increasingly recognize that it will take far too long for us to understand every aspect of life's complexity and self-organization. What we can do is know how *not* to do harm. We can know what could possibly do harm and avoid it.

I feel the best way to bring health back to the honey bee is to give it back its ecological spaces, its right to this amazing planet. I think the second thing we could do is what we wish to do for ourselves. If we think we need to eat the right food for our health we have to make sure that the crops we grow in our field and the way we grow those crops in our field is good food for the honey bee. What makes us healthy makes the honey bee healthy. I think the sacredness of many species in India, including the cow, the snake and the bee, is based on the recognition that they are vital to the web of life. And in modern ecology we talk about keystone species. In culture the way to protect keystone species is to make them sacred, building protection for them through reverence.

In my region, in the central Himalayan region of Utrantial, every home has honey bees. They have a hole in the wall; and for these people that hole in the wall is as good as building a temple. It's partly because they recognize the value of the bees to pollination. But it's also connected to the Indian healing system of Ayurveda, the science of life; and in Ayurveda, pure honey from the honey bee is one of the most healing substances. Every medical treatment includes it. And in fact, traditional healers have been extremely and rightly concerned about the introduction of Bt crops, about what that will do to the healing capacity of the honey that they prescribe.

Well, you know I come from a culture where the human species is not a special species at all. We believe in transmigration of souls. We believe that today you are a human and tomorrow you could be an earthworm and the day after you could be a honey bee. And it's precisely because of that continuity of life that we do not have the right not to care about honey bees or cows, that we care if the tiger and the elephant become extinct. We do not believe it unimportant if the whale disappears as long as we are producing enough for our own consumption. In the larger scale of cosmic evolution, that's a stupid way to think.

You know, what's called the world food crisis is actually a contemporary phenomenon. We've never used the word 'world' in association with the term 'food crisis' before because food scarcity has always been localized in space and time. Rain might fall or fail in a particular area, and that year you don't have a crop — but next year you will. You might have a war in a particular region, a little bit of food scarcity. But the permanence and globalization of the food crisis is a result of the acceleration of industrialized agriculture in the last century, and globalization of the food trade in the last decade and a half.

Both have meant huge transformations in agriculture. To begin with, there is the loss of the farmer's care for his piece of land where biodiversity thrives, where good food is cultivated, and food is not just cultivated for humans but also for the animals, for the bees. I don't think people realize that the best, ecological farming also produces food for soil micro-organisms, food for pollinators, food for farm animals, and food for the families on the farm; and only what is left over is then sent to market. After all, the market is very small compared to the number of species that have to be fed by our handling of the land. The food crisis

today where millions are denied their right to food is not a production problem in terms of not having enough food on the planet, but a distribution problem. We're putting 70 per cent of foodstuffs into animal feed for imprisoned animals, and more and more into running cars (biofuels). This automatically increases food prices. But the solution to this is thought to be to turn even more of the habitats, which we call wilderness, which are exclusively for other species – like the Amazon rainforest and the Indonesian rain forest – over to cultivation for human consumption.

The madness of constantly stealing the resources of other beings is part of the food crisis. The food crisis is not just a crisis of human entitlement to food; the human

entitlement to food is being harmed because we have first denied other species their right to food.

Our organization Navdanya promotes biodiversity. The name means 'nine seeds', and is very consciously chosen to reflect the nine planets. When we farm we are farming in ways that maintain the cosmic balance, maintaining the earth balance, and maintaining our health balance. All three are deeply interconnected. I do not think we can solve this food crisis without making two major transitions. Firstly, we must recognize, as it says in one of the Upanishads, that everything is food; everything is something else's food, and the highest sacred duty is to provide food in abundance and bounty and safety to all beings in your sphere of influence. Not just your child, but *all beings in your sphere of influence.* We still have traditions in some villages in India where a bell is rung to ask if anyone is still hungry and where the family will not eat until they have first fed the cow, the hungry person on the street, the dog and of course always some food is left for the ants. Even those beautiful mandalas that are made in front of Indian huts are actually food for the ants. And the crops that you have on your farm, in your fields, are also crops for the pollinators. All highly diverse farming systems increase food for pollinators, provide safe space for pollinators. And solving the world food crisis means solving the puzzle of how food is involved in the web of life and how the connecting species in that web are the bees and pollinators.

My very simple message to the stewards of seeds is that they are also the stewards of bees. Every seed keeper is a beekeeper. All the people in all cultures who gather and save seeds are the keepers of life, of abundance. The seeds and the bees need each other. And all of us need every creature in the great web of being.

Note

1. *Bacillus thuringiensis*; see articles by Jeffrey Smith and Vandana Shiva.

114

THE FOOD CRISIS AND THE CONNECTION WITH BEES

Interview with Raj Patel

The food crisis has a long history. It's too often forgotten that as recently as 2006 there were 850 million people going hungry, and that hundreds of millions of people have been malnourished throughout the twenty-first century. As the century wears on, that figure is going up, not down. We had over a billion malnourished people in 2008, and the number is creeping up once again in 2011. The forces tipping us into hunger are both short- and long-term. The price of oil is high, which drives up the cost of producing and shipping food. Biofuels policies in the USA and Europe mean that it is sometimes more profitable to set fire to corn than eat it. Hundreds of millions of dollars are bet in the casinos of commodity speculation. Chaotic climate events wipe out entire harvests. Meat consumption drives up the price of food too.

The food crisis has, sadly, become an opportunity for what Naomi Klein in her book *The Shock Doctrine* calls 'disaster capitalism'. The crisis has provided an alibi for industrial agriculture corporations to push unsustainable kinds of farming, for their own profit. They offer a roster of products that they claim will save farming from the abyss: genetically modified crops and farming technologies that use more fertilizer and water, and demand new land for large-scale monoculture. The trouble with monoculture is that it's the opposite of how an ecosystem works. It's farming for idiots. What you do in a monoculture is take your vibrant ecosystem, destroy it and then artificially replace all the things you just took out. So, instead of having natural mechanisms to fertilize the soil you add inorganic fertilizer. Instead of allowing a natural insect ecology to develop, you have to use pesticides. Instead of groundcover crops, you get weeds and use herbicides.

Bees are collateral damage in industrial agriculture's war on nature. The mainstream solution to the hunger crisis destroys ecosystems. At the same time, of course, this destroys the habitats and insects that make natural ways of growing food possible. And this is the disaster that corporations are ready to force on us, that they are ready to inflict on the whole world in the name of remedying the food crisis and turning a tidy profit.

Plants need pollinators, but the industrial agricultural model has a fix for that too. We had a scene from a horror movie playing out in Sacramento recently in which a truck carrying ten million bees jackknifed on the freeway, releasing a thick cloud of bees over the interstate. You might ask why bees were riding in trucks on Highway 99. Well, bees are now commodities. They've been transformed into things you can buy in boxes. Just as you can buy pesticides to kill insects, farmers rent bees to pollinate one crop or another. Now that's an example of the transformation of a rich ecosystem into a monoculture and into an engine of profit, rather than something that is a natural part of the environment. Industrial agriculture recognizes the importance of bees but it can never pay enough to replace the ecosystem services that bees offer. The almond crops, for example, are pollinated by imported bees. Although most cereal crops are wind pollinated, the ecosystems around them depend on insects – and by heading towards a pesticide-intensive agriculture you are in fact destroying bees and thus not only the basis for pollinating those crops but the entire life of an ecosystem. What we need is a shift to a different kind of agriculture and we need it desperately if we're going to feed the world.

Demographers predict that there may be ten billion people on earth by the end of the twenty-first century; and recently Robert Watson (the scientist who headed the Intergovernmental Panel on Climate Change, the most rigorous assessment of scientific knowledge on that subject) convened a group of experts called the International Agricultural Assessment on Knowledge, Science and Technology for Development. The panel's name is, admittedly, a bit of a mouthful, but what they found was absolutely inspirational. They've weighed up the possibilities of how we're going to feed the world in the future and discovered that by 2050 we're not going to be able to feed the world by industrial agricultural techniques. Nor with genetically modified crops, at least if they fail as spectacularly in the future as they have over the past 20 years. So what is

it that they propose as a replacement? They propose agro-ecological systems. Systems that are local, that work with a local environment, that actively nurture a population of insects such as bees to create a balanced ecosystem, and that provide the mechanisms for pollination without any external inputs at all.

Now that's how we're going to feed the world in the future. Not through the farming of the madhouse but by the sane farming of agro-ecology in which bees play a vital role. Cultures around the world have for millennia understood that we are one small part of an entire natural system, that we are specks in the cosmos and that we need to be humble in the face of the bounty, the beauty and ferocity of nature. Given this, it's striking that the people who rail against industrial agriculture are told they are backward, pining for something that's sort of hokey, when the best science on earth points us towards the direction so many civilizations arrived at quite early on. We are creatures in a vast web of life, and the way to feed ourselves is by respecting that web, not by tearing it to shreds. That means respecting not only the air, the earth, water, the rich ecology of the soil, but the living ecologies above it. And again, part of that ecosystem means insects and of course bees. So I absolutely think that the way we are going to feed the world involves a reconnection to our place in the cosmos, and that in and of itself this is a beautiful, powerful, rich and wonderfully empowering thing.

One of the reasons why we have a culture of scientific enquiry that is so tilted against understanding this web of life is because of the gradual takeover of the scientific establishment by corporations. Today, scientists find a pot of money at the end of the rainbow only if they ask the kinds of questions that can be commercialized. Thus the kind of questions that become the subject of scientific enquiry are 'Gee, what would happen if I twiddled with this gene or would I be able to capitalize on this particular part of the plant?' So there are lots of 'What if I do this or that?' but there's never enough of 'What would *happen* if I do that?' What will happen to the ecosystem if something intrinsically alien is released into it? What happens to nature if we unleash genetically modified plants into the very heart of, say, the cornfields of Mexico – which is exactly what's happened. A very few scientists have asked these kinds of question – such as Berkeley professor and public intellectual Ignacio Chapela, who discovered genetic contamination of corn in Mexico, the very heartland, the very home of corn. But he's a rare exception, and one who has had to suffer persecution at the university for speaking out.

The bias within the university is to ask questions about how we can manipulate nature to make our wallets fatter. And I think we need to move away from for-profit science to for-people, for-nature science. Because I do think we need to reconnect with one another as well as with our environment. And we can't do that if all our scientific questions are merely directed towards furthering corporate interests.

Perhaps the world would repair itself as soon as the last human died. Perhaps we've already broken this ecology irrevocably. But I don't want to wait to see. I'm not going out like that. I would rather that we realized our place in the universe. I disagree with those who assert that the universe would be better without humans. On the contrary – I'm for biodiversity. We're part of that biodiversity. I'm glad that there are humans around. But I think we need to learn our place. We shouldn't become self-hating animals. We should become animals that seek to connect. I know that there's a trend, particularly in radical ecology, that's very misanthropic, and sees all humans as parasites on the face of the earth. I'm not OK with that idea. I think that's a very unhealthy way to live your life.

Capitalism is parasitic and destructive, sure, but there's nothing inherently destructive about humans or about exchange. I think the way to live our lives is by realizing that we are all part of a web of life. We're not at the top of a food chain; we're in the web of a food chain. We absolutely need to reconnect with our environment, simply as a way to find our own humility and a sustainable place in the universe. Of course, that means taking on the destructive practices of capitalism, but that's OK too. A logic that turns bees into commodities, humans into insatiable consumers, and the environment into our trashcan, is a logic we have to move beyond.

Part Three
FOR LOVE OF THE BEE

What we experience within ourselves when our hearts develop love is actually the very same thing that is present as a substance in the entire beehive. The whole beehive is permeated with life based on love. In many ways the bees renounce love, and thereby this love develops within the entire beehive.

Rudolf Steiner

THE BEEHIVE

Jennifer Kornberger

1.

The bees draft nectar zones on a map
as thin as the tissue of the sun. They gust
out of the hive, coil up into the solitary
drone of their flight paths and disappear
into furrows of sky.

I get close enough to the hive to see
the blood-red pollen sacs on the thighs
of a bee, the striped purpose, the stumbling
crawl after they land, as if weighed by the
simple grief of clover.

In the late afternoon the garden is on
heat with a deep liqueur fume, bees
make a reckless toss from the sky back
to the hive, dead bees are pushed out of
the slit opening into a tidy pile, the able
shear off into the glut of light.

Towards evening a straggle of workers
gathers on the narrow veranda of the hive,
ignoring the curfew of night they sway
minutely, reliving their chaste fumbling
with the undergarments of calendula.

At night I put my ear against
the windowless box of the hive:
They are not asleep! The whole citadel
is roaring in one amber voice
drilling an umbilicus of sound
towards the buried sun.

2.

For days the bees clot
on the outside of the hive
ripening for the swarm

the moment comes as a
thickening of the light,
they pitch above in a wild
and precise choreography

a larval flow of bees
spills from the opening
and is sucked into
the spiralling thrum

they expand into a planet
of droning atoms,
ascend into suburban space

as they pass over the house
their wordless mantra
intones the interval
between a warning
and a blessing

it enters the dark chord
of the body,
weighs the heart against
the pure scale of honey
and passes on.

BEES AND THE HUMAN HEART

Matthew Barton

As Horst Kornberger has pointed out in an earlier chapter, Rudolf Steiner suggested in lectures to builders at the Goetheanum in 1923 – to their incredulity – that bee colonies might start dying out in 80 to 100 years.[1] In 2006, 83 years after this lecture, the first signs of Colony Collapse Disorder (CCD) were reported in the USA. The origins of this strange syndrome, which has since spread to Britain and Europe, are still being fiercely debated. All sorts of possible causes have been explored in this book, such as increased use of pesticides, GM crops and electromagnetic radiation from mobile phone masts. What is clear though is that bee populations are being decimated. We have seen that the syndrome, very different from other diseases afflicting bees – such as varroa mite infestation – occurs when a colony's bees suddenly disappear, leaving at most only a queen, eggs and a few immature workers: just the bewildered (female) captain and a few deck-hands on a growing number of apian Marie Celestes. No dead adult bees are found in the hive or close by. Another unique aspect of CCD is the reluctance on the part of other scavengers in the neighbourhood (bees from other colonies, pest insects such as wax worm moths or small hive beetles) to rob the plentiful supplies of food that remain in the hive. They steer clear of its eerie void.

Professor of entomology Diana Cox-Foster, of Pennsylvania State University, spells out some of the alarming consequences of this threat to bees, which is only the latest and most severe in a long series of other afflictions bees have been suffering: 'As you know … honey bees are essential for the pollination of over 90 fruit and vegetable crops worldwide. The economic worth of the honey bee is valued at more than $14.6 billion in the US… In addition to agricultural crops, honey bees also pollinate many native plants in the ecosystem.'[2]

I am not a beekeeper but a writer and poet. I am no expert and have no answers. But the experts currently have no answers either, except that this syndrome is likely to be caused by a whole range of contributing factors. Some have drawn parallels with the HIV (human immunodeficiency virus), and it is interesting in this connection that all remaining adult bees in CCD colonies have been found to suffer from fungal infections, possibly indicating a breakdown in the bees' immune system. I'll come back to that in a moment.

Having set out the mysterious facts, I want to depart from empirical science and invoke my own fallible imagination and intuition instead. Let's just imagine bees for a moment, chanting their meditative hum around a hive in the slanting sunshine of a summer afternoon, their resonant, reverberating tone. Imagine one lifting off from the lip of the hive, finding its bearings and heading for a nearby flower – an orange nasturtium, perhaps – into whose pouch it crawls to a union of sweetness, of both giving and receiving. Imagine this summation of tranquillity, of calm, unhurried intent; of the way nature flourishes at bees' slight, tender touch. And of how they return to transform pollen and nectar in the molten core, as it were, of the hive's inward organ. A continuous flow of give and take: a life-engendering and beautifully balanced out-breath and in-breath.

Little wonder then that there are countless traditions associating bees and honey with the human heart and love. The 'honeymoon' and many other marriage traditions invoke the bees and their pure gift. During old Hindu wedding ceremonies, the bride's forehead, eyelids, ears and genitals were anointed with honey. As the bridegroom kissed the bride for the first time he would say: 'This is honey, the speech of my tongue is honey, the honey of the bee is dwelling in my mouth and in my teeth dwells peace.' In Brittany they used to tie wedding ribbons to the beehives, and in other cultures a piece of the wedding cake was often left outside the hive.

Steiner has suggested that love infuses the hive, and that the sexuality to which most other life urges itself forward is suppressed in all but the queen and a few drones – in the nuptial flight of the queen – while the rest of the colony resonates with the world around it in a kind of asexual purity of love. In her book *The Hive,* Bee (!) Wilson – otherwise a sober if engaged commentator – writes:[3]

In a beehive, love seems at once to be everywhere and nowhere. Honey is one of the most tempting substances known to man; yet the bees themselves, while surrounded by all this sweetness, have always appeared free from the burdens of lust and greed . . . For men, bees are at once the exemplification both of sex and of the denial of it. And in the denial of sex, bees have promised to teach men about a higher love than the kind which usually ensnares them in the human world.

And Steiner says, similarly:[4]

The soul element that arises in us when our hearts love, is tangibly present throughout the hive. Most of the individual bees renounce love, but therefore develop love throughout the hive as a whole. We can begin to understand their life if we realize that bees live as though in an atmosphere that is wholly infused with love.

If this is how we can understand their life, perhaps, in the face of CCD, this may cast light on their death too. Both the quotations above, from very different sources and outlooks, touch on the connection and distinction between sex and love; and, however far we may seem to be erring here from the problems besetting bees which we began with, let's pause to consider it. Briefly and very generally, sexual reproduction in the animal or plant kingdoms might be seen as a kind of universal manifestation of the love inherent in life itself, by which it perpetuates itself. There is no distinction here, at least, between love and sex: the life energies culminate in a new generation and usually in some way sacrifice the old in the process. The male drones die as they mate, relinquishing their life to fertilize the queen bee. The flower is pollinated and sets seed, marking the end of the life cycle of the originating plant.

When we come to the human being, things are very different. Along with other mammals we don't die when we procreate but, as distinct from sex, which we have come to identify almost entirely with immediate pleasure, there is something self-sacrificing about love. We can certainly love without sex. When we love we are willing, in the most extreme and fervent case, to give up our life for the one we love – for a child for instance. This soul force of love is raised above the level of physical experience and becomes a tangible though non-physical warmth and power of true perception in which we dedicate ourselves to another's well-being; in which we truly want the best for another soul.

Well, that's putting it very idealistically of course. I think we can all relate to this idealism, without necessarily being very far on the path to achieving it. In love in a human sexual relationship there is, ideally, a deep marriage between the physical body and this potentially self-sacrificing warmth of soul, so that the physical urge is raised into non-physical warmth of the heart – ennobled we could say – and allows two people to create a higher union and synthesis that resonates through every level of their being. But it is equally possible and, alas, probably more common for sex to draw the kindling power of love down into the realm of self-referential, physical pleasure, and extinguish it there,

leaving both people ultimately diminished and more alone than they were before – because the physical world is what separates us, while the spirit unites.

Where does this leave the bees? Steiner – again – speaks of honey as a marvellous substance that enables the soul to work better upon the body:

Nothing is better for human beings than to add the right amount of honey to their food. In a marvellous way the bee really sees to it that we learn to use our soul to work upon our bodily organs ... the beehive gives us what we need to ensure our soul works industriously on our body ... beekeeping therefore contributes very significantly to civilization, because it strengthens us ... When we look at a beehive we should say to ourselves, with something akin to exaltation, that the whole universe enters us through the beehive, and makes us more capable human beings...[5]

Steiner, I hasten to add, is far from alone in his praise of honey, which is known in countless traditions throughout the world as a precious and also medicinal substance, as Kerry Grefig has highlighted in her essay. But he does, as often, pinpoint a fascinating aspect. As sub-text to his words above we can recognize that civilization, if it deserves the name, depends on the soul working upon and enhancing the body; and honey, a substance that the bees have first gathered tirelessly and then alchemically transmuted within the hive – which it is hard not to see as an image of the heart – apparently aids this transformative work.

But where is this taking us? I'm very tentative here, because I really do not know, and any suggestions I make are completely non-authoritative. As stated above, some experts have compared CCD with HIV: a breakdown of the bee community's immune system, leaving it exposed to all kinds of debilitating infections. HIV is of course connected with or passed on by sexual transmission, and – going out on a dangerous limb here – I could imagine that the extent of loveless human sex in the world might have some connection, in a most generalized, non-individual way, with the spread of HIV. Before I'm shouted down, let me clarify that I mean this in the most global terms: as a universal weakening of soul warmth in the world. I expressly do *not* suggest that any individual suffering from HIV has in any way brought it on him or herself. Nor am I prudishly castigating sexuality as such. I see this phenomenon, rather, as embedded in a rampant materialism that is trying hard to deny the soul and drag it deep into a cold, subhuman realm: the opposite of love.

If the HIV–CCD analogy has any mileage at all, then it is just possible that those marvellously sensitive creatures the bees, so finely tuned to their environment – which includes the human environment (and remember that human beings have always felt a particularly close connection with bees, and that it used to be thought wise to 'tell' the hives of anything important going on in the human community, such as a birth or a death) – may also be sensitive to all the negative resonances and reverberations which the human race currently emits. Underlying all of these is a soul-devoid materialism; but its effects are manifold. They include for instance electromagnetic radiation from mobile phone masts. In a presentation to the UK Beekeepers' Association, Barrie Trower, a scientific adviser to the Radiation Research Trust, cited the following examples: A man who bought a Georgian house in Bath found that he was sharing it with 30 nests of bees. All efforts to get rid of them failed – until the owner installed a WiFi system, at which the bees left and never returned. Similarly, when university scientists in Germany placed a mobile phone near beehives, both the weight of the honeycomb and the numbers of returning bees decreased. In one such experiment no bees returned at all. This presentation[6] goes into some detail about the possible effects of phone mast radiation on bees. But there are many other competing factors too as we have seen, such as GM crops and stress from excessive pesticide build-up. The scientific jury may still be out on the specific causes, but, for a comprehensive if general view of one aspect of the problem at least, let's return to Steiner again. Initially referring to bees, but then moving on to speak more generally about the weakening of domesticated animals over generations through excessive commercial exploitation, he says:

> When included as part of the farm, beekeeping is carried on in such a way that you hardly notice it … The hives were tended as just one of the other chores in those days, and people knew that honey was something so valuable you couldn't even pay for it. And in a certain sense this is absolutely right because under today's economic conditions everything you buy suffers from an

improper relationship between price and the actual work done … if the organization of society were healthy, then doubtless a proper price for honey would arise…

What the agricultural manager — usually not even a farmer but an accountant-type manager — will tell you about the quantity of milk obtained from cows is terrible. The manager reckons on so many litres of milk a day from each cow. Anyone who really understands the nature of a cow knows that it is impossible to get this much milk from a cow. But somehow they manage it … Calves born to cows that produce too much milk are weaker … You can observe this in the first, second, third and fourth generations … I am fully aware that if people continue like this, if a single cow is made to produce over 30 litres of milk a day, if they go on being mistreated like this, then dairy farming will eventually come to a bitter end …[7]

Here we come to commercial factors, and to a kind of greed which transgresses against nature, and weakens our domesticated creatures slowly through the generations. This too is another expression, ultimately, of lack of love, or tuned resonance with and heartfelt perception of our natural environment. 'People knew that honey was something so valuable you couldn't even pay for it …' says Steiner. Compare this with the (rightly) worried tone of the excerpt I quoted at the beginning: 'The economic worth of the honey bee is valued at more than $14.6 billion in the US.' Some things are so valuable you cannot put a price on them. Honey is one of them, and another is the soul warmth it strengthens.

But bees have been commercially over-exploited and thus gradually weakened for a very long time — beginning at least as far back as Steiner's era — in ways which contributors to this book have highlighted.

Perhaps we will never know the precise combination of causes that are decimating bees, but my view is as follows. Materialism in all its forms, which equates with lack of ensouled and spiritualized love — which is, after all, our task here if anything is — is in one way or another, or in all ways together, pulling bees down from their bright, buoyant heart-sphere and exhausting them with the cold cacophony of microwave pulsations, unnatural toxins and commercial exploitation. All this, in fact, stems from our own failure to be in tune with ourselves and our environment. The heart is an organ that mediates the dynamic flow of life fluid in us, 'hearkening' attentively to the whole organism and responding rhythmically to its needs. A hive, likewise, is a chamber in which life itself streams back and forth, in a continual warmth of movement, sustaining not just itself but the life of nature around it. Maybe the first thing we should do to save the bees is to feel and think differently, however weak this sounds. Strongly imagine, for instance, the vibrancy of a healthy hive, and in doing so invoke the heart warmth in ourselves and its shimmering interdependency with the cosmos. Johannes Wirz suggested something very similar to this in his piece. Bees and people are connected for better or worse. And at present, for the bees, it is definitely for the worse. The demise of the bees will mean far more than merely economic hardship.

A beekeeper called Bonnie Pearson is one of an increasing band of bee-beardists (people who wear a 'beard' of bees on their faces). What she writes below shows that in her case this is far from just extrovert showmanship, but gives her a sense of extraordinary connection with these creatures, similar to that described in the chapter by Michael Thiele:[8]

> Now after being a beekeeper for ten years I find I am in love with my bees! I like to wear a beard of them to get as close as I can to my beloved bees, to experience respect, trust, honesty and the intimacy of the colony. To me, it is now a very moving experience. There is the tactile experience of thousands of tiny pinchers gently attached to my face, weight gradually added. There is the sound of their flying and other audio communication. The pheromone mixture adds another dimension. But the most profound feelings that I get are harder to describe. I am overwhelmed with this feeling of letting go of every-thing else but just loving the bees. I am totally at peace and joined with the consciousness of the colony...

For some reason this brings me close to tears. It feels like a glimpse of a future renewal of harmony and intimacy between us and the natural world, in which we might be its fully conscious, benevolent custodians.

Notes

1. Dornach, 5 December 1923, in *Bees*, Anthroposophic Press, 1998.
2. Talk given before the US House of Repre-sentatives on 29 March 2007.
3. John Murray, 2004.
4. Dornach, 3 February 1923, in: *From Comets to Cocaine*, Rudolf Steiner Press, 2000.
5. Ibid.
6. Barrie Trower, 'Is Colony Collapse the Price of e.m.f. Progress?'. Presentation on 9 August 2008: http://www.mastsanity.org
7. Dornach, 5 December 1923, in: *Bees*, Anthroposophic Press, 1998.
8. Quoted in *The Hive*, op. cit.

THE *BIEN*:
THE ONENESS OF THE HONEY BEE COLONY

Michael Thiele

Bees exert a great, even spellbinding fascination. They are heavenly messengers, an expression of the wisdom in the universe, a spark of cosmic consciousness, and a gift to this world. To recognize and understand the unique nature of the bees means to recognize and understand something of our own fundamental nature. The oneness of the bee colony reveals the interconnectedness of the world, and of ourselves with the world. In what follows I want to shine some light on this relationship, and on what the bees can teach us.

This endeavour needs to include awareness of our language and mind. Today, our modern mindset all too easily perceives bees as a commodity, useful to us like a productive machine. Underlying this reductionist approach are constructs like '*worker* bee', honey *production*, pollination *services*, boxes, tools, bee suits and such. When asked to visualize bees, most of us might well see images of white boxes and beekeepers in white suits. Interestingly, the natural gestalt of bee colonies is very different. Natural bee nests are round, mostly in trees, and everything within these cavities is created by the bees. It is never opened artificially, and the comb is attached to the ceiling and walls. Comb is never removed nor shuffled around by anyone. Feral bees enjoy their natural diet of nectar and pollen. The natural being of feral colonies expresses itself without human distortions. The conventional mindset has lost sight of this dimension of the bees, as of nature in general. This mind deploys a language that is unaware of a reality outside its own projections, and is caught in a dualistic and exploitative relationship with the world. When studying the life forces of bees we therefore also need to study our own minds. I am continually surprised how subtle my assumptions about bees are, and how I need to continually evaluate my own actions and thoughts in relation to them, so as to allow them to express themselves – not impose myself on them.

As a means to stay open, I try to avoid using terms like 'beekeeping' and 'beekeepers'. I try to be creative with language. Sometimes we need to invent new words for a new approach.

A good starting point for this journey into the life of bees is the intricate and intimate relationship between the bee colony and its surrounding environment. Every creature is embedded in its habitat and we can see this very clearly with the honey bees. I find it intriguing to think of the entire flowering world in conjunction with pollinators. Both depend on one another, and together form a still greater organism, nourishing all life on earth like a mother. Bees live between heaven and earth, at that place of embrace between them where the entire atmosphere is pervaded by sunlight. This vastness is the home of the bees. They are a sun being. We can see how the fluid qualities of the air element are apparent in the shape of a bee's body. Their wing surface, enlarged 600 times, resembles the surface of an ocean with large waves and high caps, the surface rough as if from strong winds. Gravity is another force which provides orientation in their life between heaven and earth. It is a guide for the bee colony's creation of comb as it grows downward towards the earth. The comb with its hexagonal cells is mirrored in the bee's eyes with their 7,000 hexagonal, faceted lenses.

Bees' eyes are quite different from our own: they cannot focus or zoom in on external objects. We humans can turn towards any object in the world with the help of our flexible lenses. Our consciousness can move from within to the outside world of light, colours and objects. Bees, on the other hand, simply receive the light. The light streams through their open eyes into their body, almost as if they were merging with the visual world. Their breathing organs have a similar quality. Human lungs are an interface between the outer environment and our inner organs. Bees, in contrast, have a tracheal system which enables the outside air to reach every single organ and tissue directly through small channels within the bee's body. The ocean of the air reaches every part within. In these examples of air and light we find that there is no substantial separation between the bees and their environment. It is as if they are one with it,

so that the outer world is an extension of their interior.

Just as we come to realize how intimately the bees are connected with their environment, we discover that the colony as a whole is organized as a separate, single entity. All physical life forms are defined by a membrane, such as our skin, separating the inside from the outside world. This membrane makes life in a physical form possible, as it enables all life forms to control their inner milieu. The bee colony as a whole reveals these same features. The bees as a single organism control all aspects of life in the hive and maintain a constant temperature within, summer and winter alike.

Due to this homeostatic environment, we can imagine an invisible membrane surrounding the core of the hive. The colony is 'embodied' within this virtual and functional membrane, in a space inhabited by individual members, the bees. The colony becomes one entity, one body or creature composed of 50,000 individual bees, which act like the somatic cells of multicellular creatures. The biological term for this is super-organism; the super-organism overarches the individual parts and is more than their sum. This is evident in that a single bee is not able to survive by herself. The old German word *Bien* is an attempt to describe this oneness and define it as one being. The *Bien* is one being in countless bodies. The colony is both a society of thousands of individuals as well as one super-organism, and thus two fundamentally different systems which merge and depend upon one another. The multitude of all the single bees creates one being with capacities far beyond those of each individual bee. The *Bien* is the overall environment which raises the single individual into a higher life form, in which formerly autonomous entities are forged into a new gestalt. As a highly evolved matrix of life, the *Bien* can also be seen as a prefiguring of future human capacities of conscious and harmonious cooperation between distinct and separate individuals.

The *Bien's* largest internal organ is the comb. Bees are able to create wax out of themselves and form wax comb, where they spend about 90 per cent of their life. The comb is the location for various functions and physiological properties, the skeleton of the *Bien*, and the place where pollen and nectar are metabolized into honey and bee bread. All the individual bees are raised in a social uterus/womb. The comb serves as a communication platform, the comb-wide-web, for the famous waggle dance. Comb is also part of the *Bien's* immune system, containing microbiologically active propolis, and has symbiotic fauna in the same way that we do in our intestines. And last but not least, comb is the hive's memory organ. The entire life of the *Bien* is documented in the construction of comb and all the scents inside it. Even as the bees move around on the comb in darkness, they know exactly where they are by the scents in the wax. The wax and comb are a reflection of each colony's environment: every variety of flower and tree, soil quality, climate and sun exposure will give it a unique imprint. It is a sculpture of the surrounding flora, of the particular location where the bees live. Comb is essential and co-evolved with the bees. It is their birthright to build their own comb.

Once I began to fully understand the importance of natural comb, I could no longer move frames of comb the way I once did. How could I change what was created by the *Bien* in a certain sequence? Lately I have been wondering about incorporating feral nest conditions into apiculture. Interestingly, while bees belong to the realm of insects, the *Bien* super-organism portrays various mammalian characteristics. For instance, the body temperature of the *Bien* and of the individual bee can range from 35 to 43 Celsius (95–110° Fahrenheit). Also, it has low numbers of offspring (swarms) and the *Bien* feeds its constituent entities with nourishment provided from internal glands. This 'mother's milk' in their case is royal jelly; we should rightly call it 'sister's milk' since the sister honey bee and not the queen bee feed the larval bees. There is a threefold feature of the *Bien*, consisting of the queen, the female bees, and the drones; and these can be seen as three fundamental functional principals of life, and three ways of being. We can find them in embryonic development as the three germ layers (primary tissue layers) of endo-, meso- and ecto-derm. All body tissues arise out of these. Once we are aware of the oneness of this super-organism, we realize that the *Bien* breathes as one, maintains one social uterus, possesses one skeleton (comb) and maintains one collective metabolism.

The warmth of the *Bien* reminds me of catching a swarm one spring day. For some reason I decided to use my bare hands to move them off a branch. I used neither a veil nor smoke. I talked to them and very slowly I started touching the outside of the swarm cluster. It was as warm as my

hands. I very slowly pushed my two hands into the swarm until my palms were filled with bees. It felt like holding a liquid and warm body in my hands. At the same time it felt as though someone were touching me right inside my heart. The way the bees and I were relating with each other at that moment was a language without words. It felt as if love were pouring into my heart. I had touched a sentient being, and it was touching me too. Ever since, the *Bien* has changed my perception so that I live with bees in an entirely new way.

Another fascinating aspect of the *Bien* is the differences expressed in the two genders. The queen emerges from a long ellipse-like cell, surrounded by her court of bees who protect and nourish her. She bonds the individual bee to the oneness of the *Bien* through scent. The queen sustains the *Bien's* genetic lifeline. As the only fertile female, she is essentially a zygote and the carrier of its light, guiding it throughout the season and ushering the swarm to confidence during swarming. One could say that the queen is the guardian of the *Bien's* integrity between one 'incarnation' and the next.

Next we have the female bees. We can consider them as the *Bien's* somatic cells. Born in smaller, hexagonal cells, their life cycle develops around age-specific tasks and ranges from nursing the young, forging comb, protecting the entrance, through to foraging miles away from home. All is done in cooperation with all others in selfless service towards the whole. Their work is the foundation for future generations of bees. The honey stored this summer will feed the early offspring of the following year. Interestingly, female bees

have a very 'yang' or masculine quality. They carry the potential for bold and bellicose energy in the form of their stinger and venom. Used to protect the colony, this force is only exercised in defense, and by doing so of course a bee will sacrifice her life. Her stinger cannot be retracted from mammalian skin: the bee's abdomen will rupture, sundering the stinger from the bee and she will die shortly after. Imagine the world if this were true of human warfare.

Finally we come to the drones. The male bees are born in the largest hexagonal cells. They start leaving the hive in the early afternoon; their loud, deep flying sound is what gives them their name, and what makes their leaving the hive very noticeable. Their attributes accentuate fertility and sensitivity. Their eyes are so large that they almost completely engulf their head. As part of the sense organ of the *Bien*, they are not involved in the tasks of the female bees. Drones engage in social activities and forage for information. Through their ability to enter other bee colonies, they play an important role in connecting colonies, ensuring genetic diversity, and sharing information. They are part of a larger networking system. Drones do not have a stinger, and the male energy of the *Bien* does not appear with the typically aggressive potential associated with *yang* energy. Drones can be understood as ambassadors of peace who play a vital role in the wellbeing of the super-organism. They are an integral part of the *Bien*, and any kind of manipulation of the drones affects the entire colony (see also the article by Jacqueline Freeman). A few drones will mate with a virgin queen during her nuptial flight. Those who do so will lose their life in the act of mating. Through this selfless act, their individual life is given completely to the *Bien*. Come autumn, the drones vanish and the colony will overwinter without any drones. The male aspects of the organism, one can say, retreat from embodied existence only to reappear in the spring, and are thus attuned to the earth's natural cycle of flourishing and withering, whereas the annual bio-rhythm of the queen and the workers is more attuned to sunlight. The winter solstice marks the beginning of the new bee season, when the *Bien* starts to grow. Thus, in response to ever-increasing sunlight, the queen begins to lay eggs and the numbers of bees increase, whereas drones only appear much later, when spring begins. In the same way that the habitat of the *Bien* is located between heaven and earth, so these two poles are also represented in female and male bees.

As we have seen, bees give themselves completely to the well-being of the *Bien*. Their physical existence is completely devoted to its prosperity and survival. In the altruistic gesture of self-sacrifice we can see the extent to which bees transcend their individual existence. In fact, their sense of self includes all the other bees, encompassing the entire *Bien*. One may wonder whether the bees' sense of a group 'I' is experienced in a mode of consciousness far removed from our own rational consciousness: as a dance of all elements of the *Bien*, a harmonious dance of all individual physical elements and energies. The wisdom at work in the colony can easily begin to resonate in our own hearts. The *Bien* can become a metaphor for interconnection between ourselves and the world, making the unity of our life palpable

for us. The *Bien* can change our sense of who we think we are, and instil in us a wish to serve a higher good.

In this respect, it is interesting to discern similarities between the *Bien* and monasteries. The trinity of unity, love and service of the *Bien* is formalized in monasteries as a striving for selflessness, for renouncing ego, for serving the totality of life. The rules of St Benedict are one example, enshrining principles of the religious life as the renunciation of one's own will and pursuing a dedication to service. Another reminder of the *Bien* can be found in the *Guide to a Bodhisattva's Way of Life*.[1]

> Work towards perfect awakening, and love others before yourself, following Dharma. Practise discipline and remember your spiritual goal — you do it for the benefit of all living beings. Just as the hands and the like are cherished because they are members of the body, why are the embodied beings not cherished in the same way, for they are the members of the world?

The closer we look, the more we can discover multiple contrasts within the *Bien*. In various ways we can perceive how the individual bee can be both a self-contained insect and at the same time a cellular part of the oneness of the *Bien*. We can see the non-separation between the individual bee and the element of the air and realm of light. In contrast to this, the *Bien's* entity distinguishes and separates itself with an invisible membrane. Comb is first of all an inner organ of the *Bien*, and at the same time can also be regarded as the outer environment of individual bees. In the end, our viewpoint will determine what we call 'inside' or 'outside' – in a way reminiscent of the polarities of light, which can be understood as both wave and a particle. The merging of opposites, and the bees' intermediary existence between worlds of many kinds, makes the *Bien* into a unique creature.

The bees are a melting pot for paradigms, thwarting any easy attempts at categorization and asking us, ever anew, to come into flow in our thinking and feeling. The *Bien* joins what seems separate (spirit and matter, wave and particle), and can open the heart to a new sense of self. This goes far beyond linear thinking and can inspire and open our mind. The way we see the world is only one model of reality. The *Bien* encourages us to stay open for the vastness of existence. This depth, this inner relationship to the *Bien*, is a gift our ancestors knew how to value.

Once we understand the deeper nature and relevance of bees, we may consider how to approach them in a meaningful way. How do we relate to the *Bien*, and what kind of communication can be established? Smoke and veil are conventionally used. There is a long-held belief that smoke calms bees, while the veil is a safety precaution. Smoke does make them *appear* calm, and uninterested in the actions of the human in the veil, but this is only because it acts as a trigger of their response to one of the colony's greatest natural threats: forest fire! Smoke triggers alarm within the colony, disrupting and ending all normal activity, including that of defense. All activity shifts towards preparing for the worst and for abandoning their home. Bees start engorging honey, and prepare to flee. Unfortunately the use of

smoke goes largely unquestioned. It is the default means of interaction with the *Bien;* and with it comes a loss of connection. Anyone interested in a more intimate relationship with the *Bien* may experiment with using less and/or no smoke. This can lead to a tremendous shift in the relationship between bees and humans. The veil is an important tool to protect oneself, and yet it also carries the danger of blinding the wearer. Beyond protection, it enables the wearer to enter a very sensitive territory within the *Bien*, vulnerable areas such as the 'womb' area. The risk of this empowering tool thus lies in the fact that it has the tendency to violate our sensitive communication with bees, allowing us to think that bees can be treated like a machine, manipulated at our discretion. Due to this kind of approach, we may miss the opportunity for a true meeting with the bees.

The vast majority of bee colonies have to live with plastic foundation. This is a blueprint of hexagonal cells and comes in rectangular sheets. Plastic foundation is made of carcinogenic ingredients such as benzene. The entire *Bien*, its metabolism and uterus, will be exposed to this plastic. It is an implant which forces the bees to build cells in a non-natural size. The plastic foundation will not allow for larger cells for drones, and so the *Bien* will end up with extremely low numbers of male bees. The entire organism is affected by this, and the implications of this for propagation, genetic diversity and internal harmony are enormous. At a physical level, it fails to respect their instinctual needs and inner wisdom.

Imagine a different sort of meeting with

the bees: one centred on communication, respect, reverence, mutual exchange and curiosity. This path begins with learning the language of the *Bien* and with enhancing and fine-tuning all our senses. One of the first communication platforms is the realm of scent. The world of the bees is dominated by the olfactory sense. Therefore we need to be aware of our own scent. Strong perfume or combustion-engine exhaust on clothing will have a negative effect on the encounter. Similarly, bees are very sensitive to our mood, and the *Bien* knows exactly how we feel. That is why it is so essential to be aware of one's feelings and to respect one's own comfort level. If we are fearful, they know. The more genuine we are, the more they can relax. That is one reason why I speak and sing to

them. Not relying on smoke and veil (you can wear one if you wish, but stay awake) will give us no option but to be present in the moment and to stay open.

I also recommend horizontal hives (golden hives, top-bar hives and horizontal log hives) for this approach, because they preserve the colony's intact integrity (see chapter by David Heaf). To stay open to various levels of perception involves all our senses: visual, auditory, olfactory, thinking, feeling, intuition and imagination. When I am with bees, I like to think of entering into dialogue with the *Bien* from the moment I decide to visit them. In the proximity of the bees, I try to move as if I am literally part of the extended *Bien*.

On late spring afternoons, when bees are flying in large numbers, I sometimes

approach them carefully and move right in front of their nest entrance. Soon an increasing cloud of bees will form and hover all around me. The flying of many hundreds of them sounds almost like music. It feels like being within this being. It can bring rational thinking to a standstill. I close my eyes and just listen and surrender – surrender to a wordless world.

The *Bien* presents us with the opportunity to become quiet and to listen. Listening can be a part of being with bees. And in listening, we can practise non-knowing. Not to know presents us with the possibility of learning something new, of opening the mind to the magnitude and oneness of life, with a new sense of our own true nature. The bees can show us that our life does not end where our skin does, but extends into the environment. This new sense of self can have a radical impact on the way we walk on the earth.

Apiculture can become a spiritual path, a journey into the great fullness of life, and it can deepen our personal practice of meditation. The *Bien* can be a kind of apitherapy for the soul and inspire us at many levels. In his bee lectures, Rudolf Steiner describes the *Bien* as imbued with love-pervaded life. To meet them at that level, and to be touched by them, will show a new way of being with bees and a new way of being in this world. To ensure the harmony between bees and apiculturists, living with bees was ritualized in past eras. In our de-ritualized world, we face the challenge of finding the means to reconnect with different aspects of life and of finding guidance for being with the *Bien*.

Life on earth is in transition at all levels. In this pivotal time, the bees have entered our awareness worldwide through their struggles. Honey bee sanctuaries such as the Melissa Garden are marking a change in our cultural, emotional and agricultural landscape. Apiculture is beginning a transformation towards a wholesome way of living with bees. New voices are emerging. The *Bien* is calling.

In his bee lectures, Rudolf Steiner concludes that '...we need to study the life of bees from the standpoint of the soul'. In the end, the world shows us whenever the soul element is missing in our lives. The current plight of the bees is showing us the repercussions of our shortcomings. The bees are reflecting back to us our own struggle to live in this world. Their encouraging message is to wake up – to this fragile, wonderful and precious world. May we all wake up!

Note

1. By Shantideva (685–763), a great Indian master, scholar and bodhisattva.

SWARM SONG

Jacqueline Freeman

I find them low on a branch
an elongated football shape
10,000 strong, each atop the next
with the queen in the middle
protected, sheltered,
bees so full of honey they couldn't bend
their fat little bellies to sting if they wanted to.

I wrap my hands around the bottom-most bees
three hundred at a time, the whole living
ball of them
thrumming inside my hands
my palms vibrating with life

I place them in the hive
gently gently
One flies up
meets me eye to eye
she asks a thousand images of me
friend or foe?

Humming the sound of calm intent
thrumming inside my hands
The chorus echoes through my bones.

ABOUT THE CONTRIBUTORS

MATTHEW BARTON is a translator, writer and poet living in Bristol, UK, and the copy-editor of this volume. He has a particular interest in writing about the natural world, and was twice winner of the BBC Wildlife Poet of the Year award. His two volumes of poetry are: *Learning to Row* (Peterloo 1999) and *Vessel* (Brodie Poets 2009).

CAROL ANN DUFFY, CBE, FRSL, is a Scottish poet and playwright who '...has achieved that rare feat of both critical and commercial success' (British Council). She was appointed Britain's Poet Laureate in 2009, and is Professor of Contemporary Poetry at Manchester Metropolitan University. She has received many awards for her numerous poetry collections, including the Dylan Thomas Prize, the Whitbread Award and the T.S. Eliot prize. Her latest collection, *The Bees* (Picador), has just been published.

JACQUELINE FREEMAN is a biodynamic beekeeper and a 'bee listener', and runs her family farm, Friendly Haven Rise, in Clark County, USA. She is gifted in perceiving Nature intelligences, particularly the honey bees. Her book on honey bees is due for publication imminently. See further at www.BeesTheOtherWay.com.

KERRY GREFFIG has a background in small-scale, diversified organic farming and in nature-based education. She received her BS in Environmental Studies from SUNY Environmental Science and Forestry, and her MPS in Agricultural Extension from Cornell University. She currently lives in Sullivan County, NY, where she works as a beekeeper and orchardist at the Center for Discovery.

GUNTHER HAUK has been a biodynamic gardener and beekeeper for nearly four decades and is the author of *Toward Saving the Honeybee* (2002). A former college and Waldorf school teacher, he co-founded the Pfeiffer Center in Spring Valley, NY, and has led numerous workshops on biodynamics and sustainable beekeeping. He is presently building up a honeybee sanctuary with his wife in Virginia, USA.

DAVID HEAF began beekeeping in 2003 after giving a talk on genetically modified organisms to a local beekeepers' association. This led him to search for more 'bee-appropriate' ways of keeping bees. After being introduced to Émile Warré's natural comb hive, David and his wife translated Warré's book into English (*Beekeeping for All*, 2007). He is the author of *The Bee-friendly Beekeeper* (2010). See further at www.bee-friendly.co.uk.

HEIDI HERRMAN worked for many years as a conference interpreter for EU government institutions. In 1998, following a study of Rudolf Steiner's 'bee lectures', she developed a profound interest in beekeeping. She co-founded the Natural Beekeeping Trust (www.naturalbeekeepingtrust.org) in

2009, and now devotes her time to teaching. She is a biodynamic beekeeper, and maintains an apiary at her home as well as on a biodynamic farm in Sussex, UK.

HORST KORNBERGER is a writer, poet, lecturer, interdisciplinary artist and researcher in the fields of imagination and creativity. He has taught Goethean Studies, Anthroposophy and Epistemology in the US and Australia, and is the director of the School of Integral Art, where he pioneers creative and biographical writing. He is the author of *The Power of Stories* (Floris Books 2008). See further at www.horstkornberger.com.

JENNIFER KORNBERGER is a poet, playwright, artist and teacher. She co-founded the Goethean Studies Programme and the School of Integral Art in Perth, Australia. Jennifer's poetry is published in major Australian anthologies and in her own collection (*I could be rain*, 2007). In 2010 she received an Australia Council Literature Grant to develop her second book of poetry.

RAJ PATEL studied at Oxford and Cornell universities and the LSE, and is a writer, activist and academic. He holds several academic posts, and is the author of *Stuffed and Starved: The Hidden Battle for the World Food System* and *New York Times* bestseller *The Value of Nothing*. In addition to numerous scholarly publications, he writes regularly for national newspapers in the US and UK.

DR VANDANA SHIVA is a philosopher, environmental activist and the author of numerous books and scientific papers. Trained as a physicist (University of Ontario, Canada), she is the founder of Navdanya, an organization that focuses on saving and distributing native seeds to farmers. She sits on the board of the International Forum on Globalization and is a member of the scientific committee of Fundacion IDEAS.

JEFFREY M. SMITH is a leading spokesperson on the health dangers of GMOs, and the author of two bestselling books, *Seeds of Deception* and *Genetic Roulette*. He has briefed world leaders, and is an international speaker and popular guest on TV shows. He is the executive director of the Institute for Responsible Technology, a film producer as well as the author of an internationally syndicated column entitled 'Spilling the Beans'.

MICHAEL JOSHIN THIELE has been deeply influenced by the German biodynamic beekeeping movement and now teaches classes on natural and holistic apiculture in the US. He lived and practised for almost a decade at San Francisco Zen Center where he tended the monastic hives. He is one of the co-founders of a honey bee sanctuary in northern California (www.themelissagarden.com), and founded Gaia Bees (www.gaiabees.com).

JOHANNES WIRZ is a molecular biologist on the staff of the Research Laboratory at the Goetheanum, Switzerland. His current projects include an effort to develop criteria for beekeeping that do not include chemical attacks on the varroa mite. He edits the journal *Elemente der Naturwissenschaft*, and is a cofounder of Ifgene, a scholarly network exploring the implications of genetic engineering.

PICTURE CREDITS

All photos by Taggart Siegel unless otherwise specified.

Page 1: (top) Taggart Siegel by Jenny Siegel; (bottom) Jon Betz

Page 2: honey bee on borage

Page 8: honey bees in front of hive

Page 10: honey bee

Page 12: (top) Colin Fleay in Perth, Australia (featured in film); (bottom) Jacqueline Freeman, Friendly Haven Farms (featured in film)

Page 13: (top) Zan Yassin on rooftop in Bronx, New York; (bottom) Günther Friedmann in Stuttgart, Germany (both featured in film)

Page 14: (top) Taggart Siegel filming Sara Mapelli dancing with 12,000 honey bees, by Ruby Bloom; (bottom) Hollywood Theater theatrical premiere, Portland

Page 16: (top) Theatrical opening; (bottom) poster display at theater in New York

Page 20: Yvon Achard (featured in film)

Page 22: (top) honey bee in artichoke flower; (bottom) honey bee on echinacea flower

Page 24: honey bee gathering nectar

Page 26: Rudolf Steiner courtesy Rudolf Steiner Nachlassverwaltung, Switzerland

Page 28: honey bees at hive

Page 30: (top) queen bee being marked for artificial insemination; (middle) being placed in test tube; (bottom) being artificially inseminated. All images by Michelle Hwang (featured in film)

Page 34: (top) Keery Grefig with bees at Center for Discovery, by Jessie Wall; (bottom) checking bees by Jessie Wall

Page 37: (top) honey bees gathering nectar and pollen in artichoke flower; (bottom) gathering nectar and pollen

Page 38: (top) honey bees gathering nectar and pollen in sunflower; (bottom) gathering nectar and pollen

Page 41: (top) honey comb; (bottom) honey

Page 43: Honey Clock by Horst Kornberger (featured in film)

Page 46: Johannas Wirz on roof of Science Building, Goetheanum, Switzerland

Page 48: various pollinators, top right by Leah Hansen

Page 49: various pollinators

Page 52: Olive Siegel

Page 54: honey bee on onion flower

Page 56: Jacqueline Freeman at Friendly Haven Farms

Page 57: Drones with honey bees by Heidi Herrmann

Page 60: David Heaf watching bees at Warre hive, by David Heaf

Page 62: (top) Ron Breland with dodecahedron hive; (bottom) top bar hives

Page 63: (top) Warre hive by Ernie Schmidt; (bottom) Norbert Poeplau with Mellifera bee hives

Page 65: varroa mite, courtesy International Bee Research Association

Page 68: (top) honey bees on Günther Mancke hive by Amanda Lane; (bottom) honey bees by Amanda Lane

Page 69: various swarms; top right and bottom left by David Heaf; (bottom right) swarm being put in hive, by Jenny Siegel

Page 72: Gunther Hauk (featured in film)

Page 75: (top) queen in nuptial flight; (bottom) drone mating and dying; both by Michelle Hwang

Page 76: (top) queen flying through drones; (bottom) drones dying after mating; both by Michelle Hwang

Page 78: (top and bottom) Gunther Hauk at Spikenard Farm Honey Bee Sanctuary (featured in film)

Page 82: honey bees on flower by Amanda Lane

Page 84: (top) bee performance at Michael School, Portland; (bottom) Ron Breland with children at Rockland Country Day School

Page 85: (top) Warren Thompson and family in New Zealand; (bottom) Warren Thompson (featured in film)

Page 90: (top) Ian Davies, Hackney, London; (bottom) Zan Yassin, Bronx, New York (both featured in film)

Page 91: (top) Majora Carter, Bronx, New York; (bottom) Ian Davies, Hackney, London (both featured in film)

Page 93: (top) removing bees from a house; (bottom) Roy Arbon with bees in New Zealand (featured in film)

Page 94: (top) honey bee drinking water; (bottom) honey bee on hand

Page 99: Taggart, Jenny and Olive Siegel at harvest time

Page 100: (top) peaches by Jenny Siegel; (bottom) fruit by Jenny Siegel

Page 108: Massimo Carpinteri (featured in film)

Page 109: Ian Davies on rooftop in Hackney, London

Page 113: blueberries by Jenny Siegel

Page 115: honey bees in flowers

Page 116: honey bees in flowers

Page 120: honey bee

Page 122: honey bees in flowers

Page 130: Michael Thiele with Günther Mancke hive, by Amanda Lane

Page 134: (top) honey comb by David Heaf; (bottom) hexagonal comb

Page 138: bees on hexagonal comb

Page 140: Olive Siegel with wildflowers